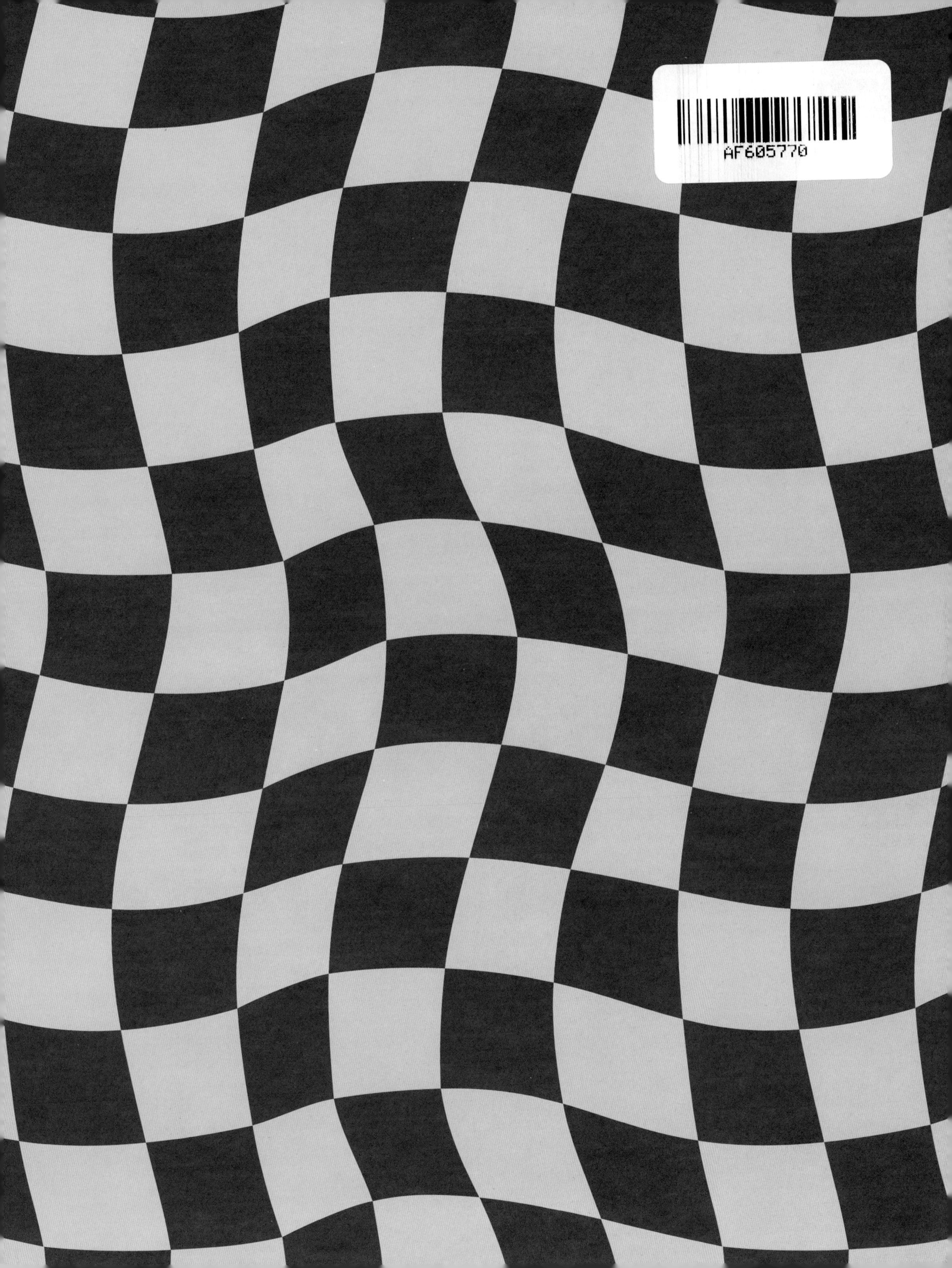

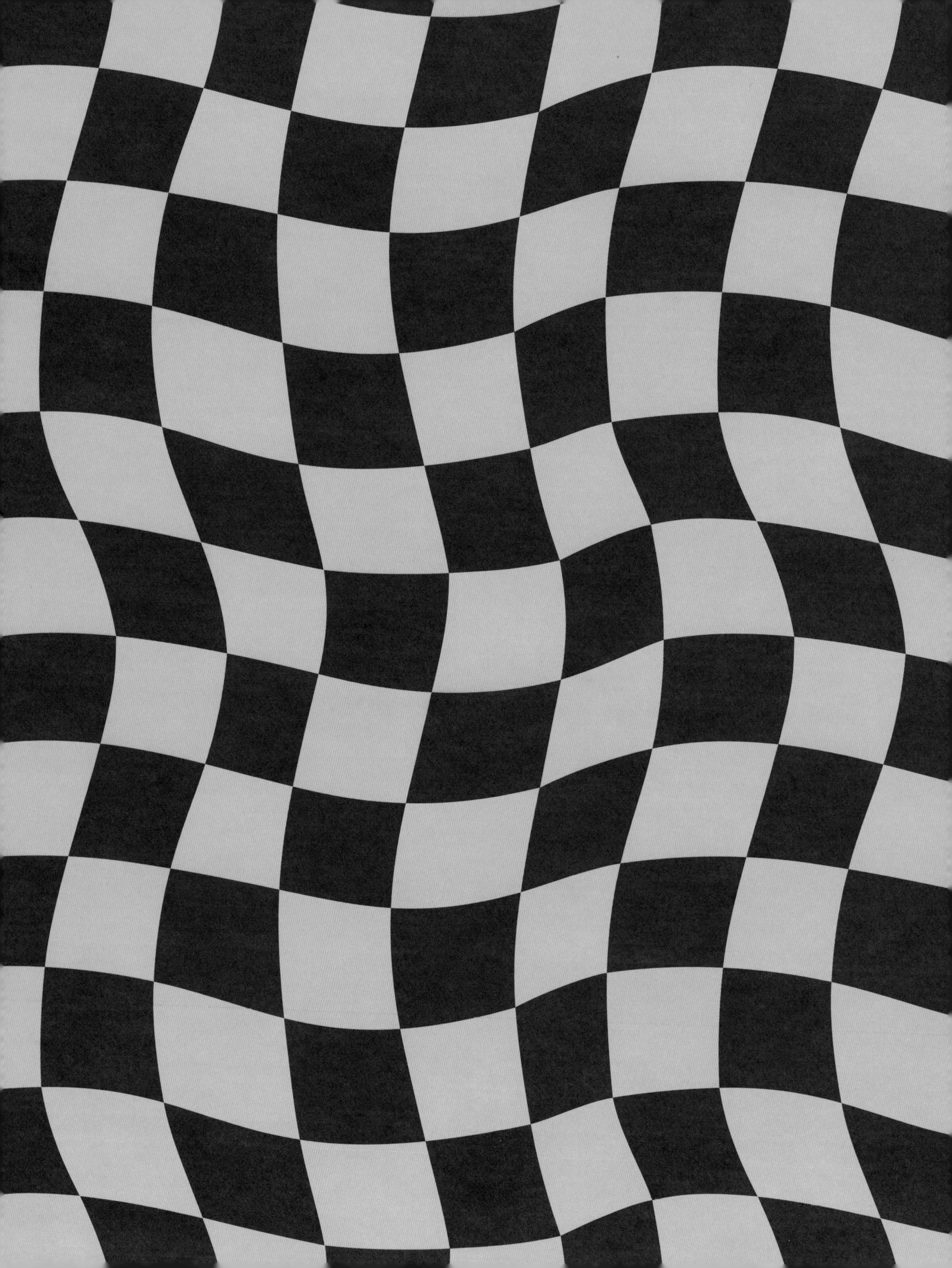

KATE JENKINSON
HALF
BAKED
LG

KATE JENKINSON

HALF BAKED

How to fool the world you can cook!

CONTORNI

Contents

There's no use crying...

Pile your carbs high!

HEY THANKS

for buying my book, but I've got some bad news for you:

I'm a sh!t cook.

Sorry, I probably should've told you that before you went and spent your money, but it's true. I'm lazy, uninspired, impatient and unprepared. And I burn things. A lot.

But the GOOD news is: If I can fool the world I can cook — then you can too!

The only thing you need is a desire to eat delicious food, and THAT'S where I come in. Because although lazy, impatient and routinely prone to burning toast, I'm also extremely greedy, and I've made it my life's mission to make food taste amazing with as little effort as possible.

I'm the Queen of Quick, the Earl of Ease and the Sultan of Shortcuts. If there's a way to feed myself with maximum flavour and minimum sweat, I've found that way and brought it to you via this book.

It all started in my Melbourne kitchen, mid-global pandemic when I decided it would be a funny idea to film myself making dinner using the scraps of sad detritus that lay in my fridge. I made noodle soup using chickpeas instead of chicken, lasagna sheets instead of pasta, crack seasoning instead of stock and sad, limp vegetables that were heading for the bin. It wasn't a fancy soup, but it hit the spot.

The more I think about it, that soup is a metaphor for me. Tired, scrappy, chaotic and thrown together at the last minute. She wasn't perfect, but she got the job done.

And that is the essence of this book, my friends. I'm not interested in striving for perfection. That takes up precious time that I could spend eating, so from my sh!t kitchen to yours, I hope you're hungry.

xx Kate

Just a quick PSA: If you find some of the language in this book confusing, it's because it is. Have a look at page 125 for a cheat's guide to understanding my kitchen language.

KATE'S FAVOURITE

Pantry Essentials

A well-stocked larder brings me inner peace, outward joy and importantly, a reason not to order Domino's. I love window shopping in my pantry, imagining what new invention I can create with the same old staples I've been buying for decades. Here are my non-negotiables.

Carbs This global crucifixion of carbs needs to stop. Carbs just want to be loved, and I love them I do. I need these on hand at a moment's notice:
Pasta. Lots of it: Spaghetti, Spaghettini, Risoni and Rigatoni are my go to's.
Noodles: Rice, Egg, Soba and Rice paper sheets.
Rice: Basmati, jasmine and Arborio. I wish I loved brown, but I don't.
Flour: Even though I'm often way too lazy to bake, I need to know I have the option. I always have Tipo 00 bread flour, plain and self-raising and yeast in case inspiration strikes.

Canned food I like the inside of my pantry to look like a maximalist explosion of preserved food. I need to know I can survive a cyclone, a global pandemic and a zombie apocalypse all at once. I always need a hefty selection of the following:
Tomatoes: crushed, whole, passata, paste.
Beans: baked, cannellini, kidney, black, chickpeas.
Corn: the only canned vegetable I can abide.
Tuna and anchovies: high quality, in oil.
Coconut milk: for curries, soups and sauces.

Dairy I'm eternally grateful to have skated through life without a dairy intolerance because I get very nervous if there's no cheese in the house. The "cheese wing" in my fridge consists of:
Cheddar: for burgers, tacos, fritters, savoury baking and paying the daily cheese tax to my dogs.
Parmesan, Ricotta and Mozzarella, for an Italian dish. Goat's and Feta, for salads and wraps. Cream Cheese for sweet baking and sandwich fillings. Cottage Cheese for health, and Halloumi because it makes me happy. I also need boat loads of full-fat milk and Greek yoghurt and cream on hand.

Lotion What the common folk call "oil". I like my food well lubricated and a variety of oils is required. I usually have a 4-litre bottle of Olive Oil at all times. It's got to be Extra Virgin and Italian. I use it often, from sautéing onions to drizzling over a martini.
Coconut oil: for curries, baking and desserts.
Neutral oils: canola, vegetable or peanut for frying. I personally don't buy into the canola or seed oil outrage, I think they're all fine in moderation.
Sesame oil: essential to make any Asian dish pop.
Chilli oil: no explanation required.

Sauces I'm pretty certain if you cut me open, sauce would spill out. I'm a saucy girl.
Tomato Sauce: Duh. Ketchup is necessary for a good life and a good burger.
BBQ: I'm a stan for a home-made BBQ sauce but I do always keep a bottle of store-bought STUBB'S.
Hot: My only hot sauce caveat is that I need a lot of it. Always. On everything. Tapatio, Cholula, Frank's Red Hot, Tabasco are my favourites.
Asian speed round: Soy (light and dark), Hoisin, Oyster, Black bean and fish are essential.
Honourable mention: Who's Sister Sheree Sauce. I'm a late-comer to Worcestershire Sauce, but she's earned her spot on the mantle.

Flavourings You can't pimp up your meals unless you have flavourings with which to pimp.
Crack Seasoning: My number 1 is Massel Chicken Style Stock Powder. I put that crack on everything.
Salt n Peppa's here and will always be here.
Everything Bagel Seasoning: Sprinkle over eggs, avocado toast, ramen, soup.
Curry pastes: Premade pastes are so good, why bother making them from scratch. I always have red curry, green curry and massaman on hand.
Special mention to Keen's curry powder. A classic.

BPA FREE
BPA FREE
FAGIOLI
ITALIAN DICED TOMATOES
400 g
PROPER
CRISPS
STOCK POWDER
MASSEL
CHICKEN
ITALIAN
HERB BLEND
HOT SAUCE
GARLIC

Something borrowed

PREP & COOK TIME 20 MINS MAKES 5 FAT BUNS

Bojana's Buns

This is the most minimal effort/maximum impact recipe I have ever come across. Three pantry staples, yep, that's it, 10 minutes to cook and the result: The warmest, fluffiest, dough-iest scones you'll ever consume. All hail Queen Bojana who stopped me while shopping one day and insisted I try her easy peasy cheesy scone recipe. She said they were life changing and I have to agree. This dough is also exquisite as a quick pizza base, or as dumplings atop a hearty stew. Thank you Bojana! Enjoy them plain, as nature intended, OR with lashings of butter, as God intended.

INGREDIENTS

1 cup self-raising flour
1 cup grated cheddar cheese (and a little extra for sprinkling)
¾ cup of milk (full-fat cow is my preference)
lashings of butter, to serve

Pimp your buns flavour combos, try paprika & Everything Bagel Seasoning, or grated apple and honey (trust me!).

SCAN TO SEE IN ACTION!

Chuck everything (except the butter of course) into a medium-sized bowl and mix until it forms a sticky dough. If pimping your buns, add your favourite flavour combo to the ingredients now; mix to form a dough. Fashion the dough into 5 balls roughly the size and shape of a dinner roll.

Evenly space your buns on a lined baking tray (or air fryer tray). Sprinkle with the extra cheese, and cook in the air fryer at 180°C for 10-12 mins.

If you're using a regular oven, make sure it's preheated to 180°C fan-forced and cook for 12-15 mins or until they look golden.

You can flip them and cook a few minutes longer if you like a crispier bun. I personally prefer mine soft and pillowy so I don't have to waste precious energy chewing.

Serve warm or at room temp with lashings of butter.

SPRING
HILL

PREP & COOK TIME 4 HRS SERVES 6

Mum's Pea & Ham Soup

This soup would be a strong contender for my last meal on earth. It's my ultimate comfort food. Rich, hearty, nutritious and delicious. I let out audible sighs whenever I eat it, as if it's relieving my anxiety one spoonful at a time. My Mum makes it for me just as her Mum made it for her. Hopefully I can convince my son to carry on the legacy. The ONLY issue with this soup is that I will never quite make it as well as my Mum does. But I'll keep trying. This soup cooks best in a multi cooker. Don't ask me why, I have no idea. I cook this soup in Clarice, which is a pressure/slow cooker for 4 hours on the slow cook setting.

INGREDIENTS

800g meaty ham hock
500g mix of yellow and green split peas
1 tbsp lotion (olive oil)
2 cups finely chopped root veg (I use potato, sweet potato, carrot)
1 onion, chopped
3 cloves garlic, minced or 3 tsp jarlic
½ cup celery, finely chopped
1 bay leaf
1 litre (4 cups) chicken stock
1 tsp crack seasoning (optional)
cracked black pepper, to taste
chopped green things (I like parsley and chives), to serve

SCAN TO SEE IN ACTION!

Wash your hock and rinse the split peas well. Add lotion to Clarice (a multi cooker) or a large saucepan over medium heat. Add your chopped root veg, onion, garlic and celery. Lay your washed hock atop your veggie base. Chuck in your bay leaf and rinsed split peas.

Pour in your chicken stock and top up with water as needed. You want just enough liquid to cover your ham hock. If you need to add extra water, I'd add a tsp of crack seasoning too. Season with pepper.

Cook for 4 hours on the slow cook setting of the multi cooker or covered on low heat in the saucepan (also for 4 hours) until split peas have completely broken down.

CAREFULLY remove ham hock and bay leaf. Remove skin, bones, and excess fat from the hock and discard. Shred the remaining hock meat and return it to your soup. Discard bay leaf.

Taste your brew to determine if you need salt or extra crack seasoning. Some hocks are very salty so this may not be required. Add seasoning if needed.

Mum and I eat this soup thick, chunky and unblended but feel free to whizz it up before adding the shredded ham, if you prefer a smooth consistency. Sprinkle with an ungodly amount of pepper and green things, if you so desire.

PREP & COOK TIME 4 HRS 30 MINS SERVES 6

Summer Spaghetti Bolognese

I wish to issue an apology to Italy as a whole and all the Nonnas therein. Sorry for stealing your beloved ragu and turning it into this Australitalian Frankensauce. My summer bolognese is about as traditionally Italian as my chihuahua Bruno, but it is, however, delicious. Perfect for deceiving the picky eaters in your family.

INGREDIENTS

1 tbsp lotion (olive oil)
1 cup finely diced veg (I use a mix of celery, carrot and zucchini, but use what you have/like)
½ onion, diced
2 cloves garlic, finely chopped
1 tomato, chopped
500g beef mince
3 big fat Italian pork sausages, skin off, torn into pieces
salt n peppa's here
1 tsp crack seasoning
½ tsp sugar
bay leaf, if you feel fancy
1 tsp dried Italian herbs
½ cup dry white wine
700ml tomato passata
500g spaghetti
grated parmesan, to serve

Heat Clarice (a multi cooker) or a large saucepan over medium heat. Put the lotion in the basket. Add all the veg, onion, garlic and tomato and let this sauté for a few minutes until it smells heavenly.

Add your beef and pork sausage, breaking up the meat so it cooks evenly. You want to get a bit of colour on your meat. A light sun tan. 5 mins is good.

Add your salt n peppa, crack seasoning, sugar, bay leaf, Italian herbs and wine. Let this bubble away for a few mins before adding the passata and giving it a good old stir.

Lock this baby away in your slow cooker, or cover your saucepan, and cook on LOW for as AS LONG AS YOU CAN. The longer you cook it the more delightful the sauce. I always opt for 4 hours.

Cook spaghetti following the packet instructions. Drain. Toss pasta through half the sauce, spoon into bowls and top with remaining sauce. Sprinkle generously with grated parmesan.

TIP It's brighter and sweeter than a traditional bol, thanks to the wine, fresh tomato and sausage. Cooking it low and slow also allows you to stash a load of hidden veg in there, because it all breaks down and melts together so no foliage remains visible.

This is a great way of using up those nearly empty peanut butter and jam jars.

PREP & COOK TIME 50 MINS + COOLING SERVES 10

Pantry Purge Granola

This recipe is heavily influenced by Nigella Lawson's epic Granola from How to Be a Domestic Goddess. One of my first and favourite cookbooks. The joy of this recipe is that you get to therapeutically cleanse your pantry of all those nearly empty packets and the result is a heavenly mountain of salty, sweet, crunchy, moderately healthy granola that is incredible on its own, or atop a smoothie bowl or even mixed into muffins.

INGREDIENTS

2 cups of your favourite nuts and seeds (see tip)
1 cup whatever dried fruit you have in your pantry (I like craisins, sultanas and apricots)
450g rolled oats
2 tsp ground cinnamon
1 tsp ground ginger
½ cup syrup (rice malt, golden or maple)
½ cup applesauce or any pureed fruit (optional, but I highly recommend)
¼ cup honey
¼ cup brown sugar
1 tsp salt
¼ cup neutral flavoured oil
½ cup any old nut butters or jam
milk, yoghurt and berries (optional), to serve

Preheat oven to 150°C fan-forced. Line two oven trays with baking paper.

Chop your nuts roughly. If using larger dried fruits like apricots, dates or peaches, give these a rough chop too, set aside.

Chuck absolutely everything into a big mixing bowl EXCEPT the dried fruit (and the serving ingredients, obvs). If you're using any nut butter that's solidified then chuck it in the microwave for 30 seconds until it's runny. Make sure your ingredients are mixed extremely well.

Spread your wet granola mix evenly between the two lined trays. Cook the granola for at least 40 mins making sure to give it a good stir half way so it cooks evenly. I like this granola quite crunchy so I often cook for up to an hour in total. As long as you keep the temp low and keep an eye on it, you'll be golden.

Once your granola has cooled down completely, toss in your dried fruit and store in an airtight container. This stuff NEVER lasts long in my house, but it'll stay good for up to 2 weeks.

Serve with milk, yoghurt and berries, if you so desire.

TIP Use absolutely anything in your pantry that looks like it could go in granola for example, walnuts, almonds, peanuts, Brazil nuts, pepitas, any and all seeds like chia, sunflower, poppy and sesame.

PREP & COOK TIME 20 MINS SERVES 2

Princess Pasta

This recipe has been shamelessly stolen (with a few alterations) from Meghan Markle, who stole it from Martha Stewart who most likely stole it from a Nonna in Italy. I was sceptical that such a simple recipe would be this delicious but it most certainly is. Meghan claims this dish is devoured by her kids and I wish I could say the same, but for now this dish is made in my house JUST FOR ME. And I feel extremely regal indeed when I'm eating it.

INGREDIENTS

2 tbsp lotion (olive oil)
1 cup chopped cherry tomatoes
2 cloves garlic, minced or 2 tsp jarlic
salt n peppa's here
2 tsp grated lemon zest
1 tsp crack seasoning
chilli flakes, to taste
250g thin pasta like angel hair or spaghettini
1 litre (4 cups) boiling water
2 cups chopped silverbeet or spinach
juice of 1 lemon
2 tbsp grated parmesan cheese
chopped green things (I like basil and parsley), to serve

Heat a large, deep frying pan on low heat. Put the lotion in the basket. Add your tomatoes, garlic and season with salt n peppa, let this sauté for around 3 mins until it smells incredible.

Increase heat to medium and add lemon zest, crack seasoning and chilli flakes, to taste. Give it a stir and lay the raw pasta on top of this mix. Add enough boiling water to JUST cover your pasta.

Once the water is bubbling, cover with a lid and let cook for around 8-10 mins, stirring a few times throughout. Once the pasta is just about ready, toss in your silverbeet, and let it wilt down slightly.

Add extra salt n peppa if you wish, a good drizzle of lemon juice and a mountain of grated parmesan.

Scatter with chopped green things and serve on your most princess-like fine china (in my case, the chipped IKEA plates I've had for 15 years).

CRUMBLE

PREP & COOK TIME 20 MINS MAKES 2

Burger King

There's Burger King and then there's THE Burger King: My wonderful Father in Law Billy cooks dinner for the family every Sunday night without fail and this is one of his greatest hits.

INGREDIENTS

250g beef mince, not too lean
salt
1 tbsp lotion (olive oil)
2 slices cheddar cheese
2 burger buns of choice (soft white roll for me)
butter, for spreading (optional)
2 tbsp mayonnaise
2 tbsp diced onion, sautéed or raw or both
4 pickle slices, dill, not sweet
squirt of tomato sauce
squirt of American mustard
2 slices tomato
½ cup shredded iceberg lettuce
salted chips, to serve (optional)

My FIL aka "The Day Bed"

Work the beef mince well with your hands, then divide into two and shape into thin patties slightly larger than your burger buns, about 2cm thick. You want the mince firmly formed so the patties don't crumble while cooking. THIN is key here because you can char them on high heat without over cooking.

Generously salt the burger patties on both sides. Heat the lotion in a large frying pan on medium-high heat; cook burger patties for 4 mins on each side, to get as much char as possible.

Place a slice of cheese on each pattie, turn the heat off and cover the pan until the burger is cooked through and the cheese has melted.

Lightly toast your buns and spread with butter if you desire.

Add a generous layer of mayo to the bottom bun, top with your cheesy pattie. Atop the pattie, add onion, pickles, sauce, mustard, tomato and lettuce. Squish the bun lid ontop and enjoy the best burger on planet earth. Chuck some salted chips on the side, if you desire.

TIPS The bread should be soft and squishable. There should be enough mustard, ketchup and mayo that you'll invariably need to wash your shirt afterwards. And some salad because I'm extremely health conscious.

CONTORNI
HOT

PREP & COOK TIME 20 MINS SERVES 4

Thank You Chicken

This recipe is more commonly known as "Marry Me Chicken" – a dish so delectable that it instantly elicits a proposal from anyone you cook it for. I decided to put this recipe to the test and see if I could secure a proposal from my long-time partner and baby Daddy. I proudly presented him with this decadent, dreamy, creamy chicken pasta, eager to hear his response, which was: "Thank you." So, not guaranteed to secure a proposal, but guaranteed to be delicious, every time.

INGREDIENTS

2 chicken breast fillets (600g) or 600g chicken thighs (I prefer thighs)
¼ cup plain flour
1 tsp dried oregano
1 tsp dried thyme
½ tsp chilli flakes
salt n peppa's here
lotion (olive oil)
2 cloves garlic, chopped or 2 tsp jarlic
½ cup sundried tomatoes, chopped
1 tbs tomato paste (optional)
½ cup thickened cream
¼ cup finely grated parmesan cheese
½ lemon, to squeeze
400g spaghetti or your favourite carb
green things (I like little basil leaves), to serve

Cut your chicken breast in half widthwise. You want your chook to be thin, like a schnitzel. If using thighs, lightly bash with a meat mallet or rolling pin.

Mix the flour, dried herbs, chilli and salt n peppa on a large plate. Dredge your chicken in the spiced flour mix, making sure everything is coated well. Shake away excess. Heat a glug of lotion in a large pan on a medium heat. Pan fry your chicken for about 4 mins each side until nicely browned and cooked through. Remove chicken, cover to keep warm and set aside. DON'T CLEAN THE PAN!

Add the garlic, sundried toms and paste, if you desire, to the pan. Cook, stirring a bit, until the garlic and tomatoes have softened. Add the cream and let this meld together for a minute or two. Add the parmesan and a squeeze of lemon.

Meanwhile, cook spaghetti following the packet instructions. Drain. Stir spaghetti through the sauce.

Slice the chicken. Spoon saucy spaghetti onto serving plates, top with thank you chicken then make it rain with green things.

Porn Corn

PREP & COOK TIME 15 MINS SERVES 4

Cook 4 shucked and de-bearded corn cobs in a large pan of boiling water for 5-7 mins until tender. Drain. Return corn to pan, add 40g butter, 1½ tsp tajin (Mexican seasoning), ½ cup finely grated parmesan and salt n peppa. Toss around until the corn is fully drenched in buttery, cheesy spice. Serve with a squeeze of lime and make it rain with chopped coriander. Enjoy!

ABOUT THIS RECIPE

Aptly named, this side dish is so salivatingly good it should be X-rated. This is my take on Mexican street corn using ingredients more commonly found in my fridge. Might not be super traditional, but it's super delicious.

Sore Jaw Slaw

PREP TIME 20 MINS + REFRIGERATION SERVES 4

Chuck 1½ cups shredded purple cabbage, 1 cup shredded carrot, ½ cup thinly sliced celery, 1 small red apple, cut into thin sticks and 1 thinly sliced green onion together in a large bowl. Shake 2 tbsp lemon juice, ¼ cup whole egg mayo, 1 tbsp Greek-style yoghurt, 1 tsp Dijon mustard and 2 tbsp apple cider vinegar in a sealed jar. Pour dressing over slaw, season with salt n peppa and toss really well to coat with dressing. Cover and refrigerate for 30 mins to let flavours meld before serving. Serve sprinkled with Everything Bagel Seasoning,

I always thought pickling veg was a giant faff around; boiling jars, making airtight seals etc. Well, you CAN do it that way, but the lazy girl method works just as well. This recipe is the saviour of many a "beige dinner." You know those meals where you SHOULD make a salad or stir fry some veg but you just can't be bothered. Grab a handful of Frickles and call it a day. These pickles work on almost ANY meal you could imagine.

Frickles (Fridge Pickles)

PREP TIME 30 MINS SERVES 8

Place 2 cups of your favourite julienned and thinly sliced mixed veg in a large pickling jar or airtight glass container. I like a mix of red onion, carrot, Chinese cabbage, cucumber, radish, cauliflower, zucchini and chilli, whatever I have on hand at the time. Add ¼ cup caster sugar, 2 tbsp fine salt, 1½ cups white or apple cider vinegar, 1½ cups water, 2 bay leaves and 1 tsp crushed peppercorns. Seal it up, give it a good shake to incorporate the flavours and THAT'S IT. Store in the fridge for up to 2 weeks.

TIP Veg can be chopped instead of thinly sliced.

IRVINE
2020
SPRING
HILL
MERLOT

PREP & COOK TIME 4 HRS 20 MINS SERVES 2

If food is the way to a man's heart, then this giant rack of sticky sweet, fall off the bone pork ribs should secure not only his heart, but his body, spirit, soul and the keys to his beloved Land Cruiser. I make these ribs for my partner whenever I want to "Get Lucky". And by "Get Lucky" I mean he will be so full of pork that he'll slip into a meat coma and I can have the couch, remote and wine to myself for the evening. Highly recommend these to anyone hoping to Get Lucky tonight.

INGREDIENTS

salt n peppa's here (½ tsp each)
1 tsp smoked paprika
1 tsp cayenne chilli powder
2 tsp onion powder
1 tsp garlic powder
1 tsp mustard powder
1 tsp ground cumin
½ tsp chipotle powder, optional
¼ cup brown sugar
1kg rack of pork ribs
1 tbsp lotion (olive oil)
Sore Jaw Slaw (see recipe page 26) and Porn Corn (see recipe page 26), to serve

SAUCE

½ cup store bought BBQ sauce
½ tsp vinegar (apple cider is my pref)
hot sauce, to taste (optional)

Bung all the spices and sugar in a bowl, and mix thoroughly. Flip your ribs bone side up and locate the papery membrane on the back of your ribs. Use your fingers or a knife to remove the membrane. This helps cook the ribs more evenly. It's a pain in the tit, but it's worth it.

Drizzle your ribs with lotion and make it rain with the spice mix, covering every nook and cranny. Massage until your hands look like you've committed a crime.

Heat a large frying pan (or your slow cooker if it has a sauté function). Sear the ribs on both sides until the meat starts to colour. Transfer to your slow cooker and cook on low for AT LEAST 4 hrs, 6 is better. Reserve all the pork juices!

Once the ribs are done, place on an oven tray and stick them under a hot grill for 10-15 mins or until you get a nice char happening.

For the sauce, transfer all of the incredible porky juices at the bottom of your slow cooker to a small pan. Add the BBQ sauce, vinegar and hot sauce, if you desire. Customise the sauce to your personal taste. If you like a super sweet sauce add some sugar or honey, for extra punch then go nuts with the hot sauce. Let the sauce bubble and thicken on a medium heat for a few minutes.

Drizzle this liquid gold over your charred ribs, serve with Sore Jaw Slaw and Porn Corn for the ultimate Yee-Haw American BBQ Bonanza and enjoy getting lucky for the rest of the evening!

Bippi
ITALIAN STYLE
CHILLI
CHOTTO MOTTO

SCANPAN

PREP & COOK TIME 20 MINS SERVES 2

Brother's Mussels

Down the road from my childhood house was an extremely dodgy, down trodden tavern which inexplicably served the best chilli mussels I've ever consumed in my life. My brother and I would order them weekly when I was home for holidays. We've spent the last two decades chasing the dragon, hoping to find mussels that good again, but to no avail. This homemade version comes close, but is still a shameful second place to that daggy, smelly pub.

Eating our way through NYC

INGREDIENTS

1kg uncooked mussels, washed and de-bearded
2 tbsp lotion (olive oil)
1 cup Saucy Minx Sauce (see recipe page 51)
1 whole red chilli, seeds in, thinly sliced
½ cup dry white wine
chopped green things (parsley) and lemon wedges (optional), to serve
crusty bread, to serve (not optional)

Make sure your mussels are thoroughly scrubbed and de-bearded. You can get your fishmonger to do this. Discard any mussels that are already open or broken.

Heat your lotion in a large saucepan on a medium-low heat. Add your Saucy Minx Sauce and sliced chilli. Cook for 2-3 mins until the sauce has warmed through. Add the wine and cook for a further 3-4 mins until starting to bubble.

Tip in your mussels. Shake them around the pan so they get doused in the sauce. Cover and cook until all the mussel shells have opened, around 6-8 mins.

Make it rain with chopped green things and serve with lemon wedges (if you're feeling zesty) and crusty bread.

PREP & COOK TIME 30 MINS SERVES 4

Recycle Rice

This creamy, mild and savoury risotto has been a favourite of mine for decades. Unfortunately for me, I'm the only person in my family who likes risotto, so I've come up with ways to reinvent this rice, such as in fritters, bowls and a not-so-authentic "fried rice", so I can literally have my cake and eat it too.

INGREDIENTS

1 tbsp lotion (olive oil)
40g butter
2 garlic cloves, minced or 2 tsp jarlic
1 small onion, diced
1 cup risotto rice (arborio)
½ cup dry white wine
1.25-1.5 litres (5-6 cups) vegetable or chicken stock
1 bunch asparagus, cut into 3cm lengths
½ cup peas, thawed
1 cup baby spinach leaves
½ cup finely grated parmesan, plus extra to serve
salt n peppa's here
lemon juice (optional)
¼ cup chopped green things (I like basil and parsley), plus extra to serve

Clarice has a sauté function, if your cooker does too, switch it on now, or heat a large saucepan over a low-medium heat. Add your lotion, half the butter, all the garlic and onion, then sauté for 3 mins until translucent.

Add your arborio rice. (I don't prewash rice for risotto because I want the starch to remain.) Stir to ensure each rice grain is nicely coated in your oily, buttery onion and garlic mix. Add your wine and let it bubble until most, if not all, the wine has evaporated.

Clarice also has a risotto function which works perfectly every time, so I add 5 cups of the chicken stock at this stage, hit risotto and call it a day. If you're cooking on the stove top I recommend adding your stock 1 cup at a time, stirring frequently, and waiting until most of the liquid absorbs before adding more. This is definitely more labour intensive, which is why I get Clarice to do it for me! Repeat until you have a smooth, creamy, porridge-like consistency. Don't feel like you have to use exactly this amount of stock listed, just eyeball your risotto and use more or less stock as needed. The rice should be cooked but with a little "bite" to it. You don't want mushy rice.

Meanwhile, blanch asparagus and peas in a small saucepan of boiling water for 2 mins. Drain.

Stir asparagus and peas into risotto with the spinach, remaining butter, the parmesan and green things. Season with salt n peppa if you think it needs it. Add a squeeze of lemon juice, if you desire. Make it rain with extra parmesan and extra green things.

EXTRA

Kindy Noodles

PREP & COOK TIME 15 MINS
SERVES 4

Heat 2 tbsps neutral oil in a large pan/wok on high. Toss in 2 portions (600g) thawed Crouching Cow, Hidden Veg mince (see recipe opposite), breaking it up with a spoon, and cook for 5 mins until browned. The trick is to not stir it too much. Add 2 tbsp each of soy sauce, hoisin sauce and honey. Add 1 tsp sesame oil and 1 tbsp sriracha (if it is for adults only). Reduce heat to medium; stir-fry for 3 mins. Add 1 bunch thickly sliced pak choy and cook a further 2 mins until sauce is thick and glossy. Meanwhile, cook 250g instant ramen following packet intructions; drain. Stir noods into mince mixture until coated in the salty, sweet, meaty sauce. Serve scattered with sliced spring onion and drizzled with chilli sauce, if you wish.

PIMP IT!!

If I'm eating these, I always pimp them with crispy chilli oil and sesame seeds. Maybe even a handful of Frickles (see recipe page 27), if I'm feeling fancy.

Sausage Scrolls

PREP & COOK TIME 35 MINS
MAKES 18

Place 3 just thawed puff pastry sheets on the bench. Spread 1 portion (300g) thawed Crouching Cow, Hidden Veg mince (see recipe opposite), evenly and thinly over the pastry sheets. Sprinkle 1 cup grated cheese over mince. Roll the pastry up like a cinnamon scroll. Brush a whisked egg over the pastry. Cut into 4cm thick slices. Place cut-side down on a lined oven tray, sprinkle with extra cheese if you wish. Cook in a preheated 180°C fan-forced oven for 20-25 mins, until golden and crispy. Serve with tomato or barbecue sauce.

FLOOR FOOD

This quickly de-frostable mince will bail you out of dinner jail every time. Tacos, bolognese, cottage pie, burgers, meatballs, sausage rolls. And of course Kindy Noodles and Sausage Scrolls. You name it, you can cook it from this mix. Basically all the things kids love to eat, and for some reason always end up on the floor.

Crouching Cow, Hidden Veg

PREP TIME 20 MINS MAKES 1.2KG (4 PORTIONS)

Very finely chop ½ onion and 2 celery stalks, add to a bowl with 2 cloves minced garlic, 1 finely grated carrot, 1 finely grated small zucchini, 1 tsp crack seasoning and salt n peppa. Add 1kg beef or pork mince or a combination of both. Use your hands to mix everything together to become one inseparable entity. Divide your mixture into 4 equal portions (300g each), store in sealed freezer bags or airtight containers in the freezer for up to 1 month. Thaw portions in the fridge overnight before using.

Eggy weggs

PREP & COOK TIME 10 MINS SERVES 2

Pimped Ramen with Tipsy Eggs

There is an elite ramen chain in Tokyo and New York called Ichiran and their Tonkatsu with jammy soy eggs lives rent free in my head. No ramen is complete without a jammy, umami, soy marinated boiled egg. In fact, no fridge is complete without Tipsy Eggs (recipe page 51). This is my extremely bastardised version of that magical elixir.

INGREDIENTS

2 egg yolks
2 tbsp kewpie mayo
2 small garlic cloves, minced
2 x 85g packet instant Ramen noodles of choice (I love Indomie Mi Goreng)
2 tsp crack seasoning
2 Tipsy Eggs, halved **(see recipe page 51)**
2 tbsp sliced green onion
crispy chilli oil and Everything Bagel Seasoning (optional), to serve

Bung the yolks, mayo, garlic and ramen seasoning sachets in a bowl. Mix thoroughly to form a paste. Divide mixture between two serving bowls.

Half fill a small saucepan with 2 cups water and bring to the boil. Add crack seasoning to make a stock. Add instant ramen noodles. Cook following the packet instructions. Reserve 1 cup liquid.

Using tongs, divide the noodles between the two bowls, give a good stir with the paste to mix thoroughly. Stir ½ cup of the reserved noodle liquid into each bowl. This will create a sauce, it is not a soup.

Top noodles with halved Tipsy Eggs and green onion, add a generous spoonful of crispy chilli oil and finish with a scattering of Everything Bagel Seasoning, if you wish. Schedule an appointment with your cardiologist, and enjoy!

Eggy Spagheggi

I once moonlit as a vegetarian for 10 years, with eggs as my main protein. One morning, with only eggs and leftover spaghetti in the larder, Eggy Spagheggi was born – a magical way to stretch leftovers into something new.

PREP & COOK TIME 30 MINS SERVES 2

INGREDIENTS

1 tbsp lotion (olive oil)
4 cups leftover Summer Spaghetti Bolognese (see recipe page 16), (see tip)
6 eggs
¼ cup milk or cream
grated parmesan, chopped parsley and Cheesy Garlic Croûton Crumble (see recipe page 51) (optional), to serve

Preheat grill to medium-high. Heat lotion in a large ovenproof frying pan (26cm, 4cm deep) on medium heat. Add your leftover spaghetti bolognese and heat through. Spread spaghetti evenly over base of your pan.

In a small bowl, whisk eggs well with milk or cream. Pour over spaghetti, jiggling your pan until the egg mix evenly coats the pasta. Cook for 8-10 mins until egg is almost set. Bung under the grill for 2-3 mins to set the middle.

Transfer to a plate, scatter with extra parmesan, parsley and croûton crumble, if you wish.

TIP Any leftover pasta works well here: Princess Pasta (see recipe page 20), Speedy Ragu (see recipe page 58) or a pesto pasta etc.

Grandma's Curried Eggs

My grandma always said she "loved HOT curry" – though in truth, it was just her beloved mild curried egg sandwiches. This recipe is my nostalgic nod to her love of curried eggs.

PREP & COOK TIME 25 MINS MAKES 6

INGREDIENTS

6 Tipsy Eggs (see recipe page 51), (see tip)
2½ tbsp whole egg mayo
20g butter, softened
1 tsp Keen's Curry powder
salt n peppa's here
1 tbsp chopped green things (I like chives)
smoked paprika and Everything Bagel Seasoning (optional), to serve

Cut your eggs in half; scoop out the yolks and transfer to a small bowl. Add mayo, butter, curry powder and salt n peppa. Use a fork to mix until smooth, light and fluffy.

Spoon or pipe your curried yolk mix back into the egg whites, sprinkle with green things, then dust with smoked paprika and Everything Bagel Seasoning, if you wish.

TIP You can use plain boiled eggs for a more traditional take on curried eggs.

PREP & COOK TIME 10 MINS SERVES 1

Calzomelette

This morsel is part calzone, part omelette. She is practical. She is delicious. She is Calzomelette.

INGREDIENTS

1 tbsp lotion (olive oil), plus extra
¼ chorizo, chopped
1 flaky roti bread (see tip)
2 eggs
1 tbsp milk or cream
salt n peppa's here
¼ cup grated cheese
a few baby spinach leaves
1 spring onion, chopped
4 cherry tomatoes, quartered
hot sauce and Everything Bagel Seasoning, to serve

You could use any toppings you like think mushrooms, bacon, feta, olives, frickles etc.

Heat half the lotion in a frying pan on a medium heat. Add your chorizo, cook for 3-4 mins until crisp; use a slotted spoon to transfer to a plate. Add your roti to the oily pan. Fry for 1-2 mins each side until fluffy and flaky. Remove roti from pan and set aside.

In a small bowl or jug, whisk the eggs and milk or cream, add salt n peppa. Add remaining lotion to the same pan, then pour in egg mixture. Tip your pan to spread the egg evenly across the base and don't stir. You want an omelette, not a scramble.

Cook omelette for 2 mins or until eggs are nearly cooked; sprinkle over your cheese. Place the roti bread on top. You want the bread to stick to the cheese and nearly cooked eggs. Cook for 1 min or until the eggs are just set. Place a plate over the pan, say a prayer and flip the pan upside down.

Scatter spinach, spring onion, tomatoes and chorizo over two-thirds of omelette. Fold the other side over filling, drizzle with hot sauce and sprinkle with Everything Bagel Seasoning. You have yourself a calzomelette.

TIP Use a thin pita bread or tortilla if you don't have roti.

The OG Pea Soup proprietors

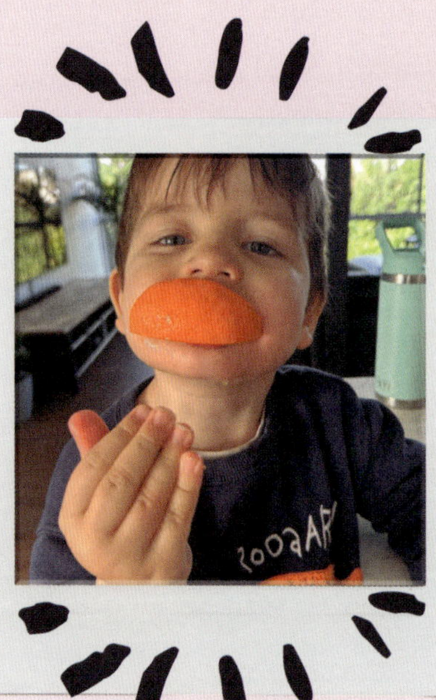

Arvo dip!

Spag Bol or face paint?

Boys do belong in the kitchen

Take me back!

Baby Daddy X Baby Mumma

The Two Sh!t Kitcheneers

The world's most expensive dog

One of us is happy for a kiss

The Nugg Life

Sure, it's a taco

RABO

PREP & COOK TIME 30 MINS SERVES 4

Mother-in-Law Quiche

This is a modern, cooler version of a Quiche Lorraine. And since my Mother-In-Law's name is Lorraine, and she is both modern and cool, this will henceforth be called "Mother-In-Law Quiche".

INGREDIENTS

1 tbsp lotion (olive oil)
3 rashers bacon, thinly sliced
1/3 cup cherry tomatoes, halved
1 bunch asparagus, trimmed
6 eggs
1/3 cup thickened cream
¼ tsp crack seasoning
salt n peppa's here
1½ sheets frozen puff pastry, just thawed
50g drained marinated goat's cheese
smoked paprika, for dusting
chopped green things (I like chives), to scatter

My MIL as the Easter Bunny

Preheat oven to 200°C fan-forced. Grease and line base and sides of a 20cm square cake pan or baking dish with cooking spray.

Heat lotion in a frying pan on medium heat, toss in your bacon and cook for 4-5 mins until beginning to caramelise and crisp slightly. Remove and set aside.

In the same bacon-y pan, add your tomatoes and asparagus. Cook for 1-2 mins until well flavoured with bacon juice.

In a bowl or jug, add your eggs, cream, crack seasoning and salt n peppa, and whisk to combine.

Place your puff pastry sheets, slightly overlapping in the greased pan or dish, gently pushing excess pastry up the side of pan, to form a shallow bowl of sorts. Pour your egg mix into shell and arrange your bacon, tomato and asparagus on top, then crumble goat's cheese over it all.

Bake for 15-20 mins or until the pastry is puffed and golden and the eggs are softly set. Stand for 5 mins then using the baking paper, carefully remove from pan.

Serve quiche dusted with a little smoked paprika and scattered with green things.

STAPLES

Tipsy Eggs

PREP & COOK TIME 15 MINS + REFRIGERATION MAKES 6

For jammy eggs, place 6 cold eggs in a saucepan of cold water. Bring to the boil and cook for 5 mins. Once the time is up, immediately transfer the eggs to an ice bath to stop them cooking. Peel. Chuck ½ cup light soy sauce, ¼ cup rice vinegar, 1 tbsp caster sugar, 1 minced clove garlic or 1 tsp jarlic, ½ tsp grated fresh ginger or ginjar and ¼ cup water in an airtight container large enough to fit the eggs. Add the eggs, put the lid on and gently jiggle it around so the eggs get thoroughly sozzled in the sauce. Stick in the fridge for at least 2 hours before serving or up to 3 days.

TIP No ramen is complete without an umami, soy marinated boiled egg. In fact, no fridge is complete without these eggs. Eat them on avo toast, in a salad, absolutely ANY noodle dish, or just on their own.

Tzatziki

PREP & COOK TIME 10 MINS SERVES 4

Chuck 1 cup full fat Greek yoghurt, 1 minced garlic clove or 1 tsp jarlic, ¼ cup finely chopped or grated Lebanese cucumber (squeezed to remove liquid), juice of ½ lemon, 1 tbsp lotion (olive oil) and ¼ cup finely chopped green things (I like mint). Add salt n peppa's here (just a pinch of each) and mix well to combine. Stick in the fridge until ready to use.

Saucy Minx Sauce

PREP & COOK TIME 2 HRS 15 MINS MAKES 4 CUPS

Heat 2 tbsp lotion (olive oil) in a multi-cooker, set it to "sauté" or heat in a large saucepan on medium heat. Add 3 minced cloves garlic or 3 tsp jarlic, 1 small chopped onion, 1 tsp caster sugar, 1 tsp crack seasoning, 2 sprigs thyme or 1 tsp dried Italian herbs and ½ tsp salt. Sauté for 3 mins until translucent. Add ¼ cup dry white wine (optional); simmer for 2 mins to reduce. Stir in 800g can diced tomatoes, 1 chopped ripe tomato, ⅓ cup water and 1 bay leaf. Reduce heat to low. Cook on LOW for as long as time will allow, 2-3 hours but at LEAST 30 mins. If cooking on the stove, cook covered on LOW heat and stir occasionally, check after 1 hour. Discard bay leaf and thyme sprigs.

Cheesy Garlic Croûton Crumble

PREP & COOK TIME 30 MINS MAKES ABOUT 1½ CUPS

Break up 4 large slices stale sourdough bread and blitz in the food processor until you get bread crumbs. You can go really chunky or really fine, per your preference. Chuck into a large bowl, then add 2 minced cloves garlic or 2 tsp jarlic, ½ cup grated parmesan or sharp cheddar, 1 tsp salt flakes, ¼ cup olive oil, ½ tsp chilli flakes (optional), a pinch of smoked paprika (optional) and mix until every crumb is coated in spice, oil and cheese. Spread on an oven tray and cook in a preheated 190°C fan-forced oven for 10 mins; stir and cook another 10 mins until golden and crisp. Keep an eye on this one. It goes from not done to burnt in a millisecond.

TIP Croûton crumble can be stored in an airtight container for up to 3 days or freeze up to 1 month.

PREP & COOK TIME 25 MINS SERVES 4

Nice-wah Salad

This is my take on the classic Niçoise. Pretty much the only salad on earth that I think qualifies as a proper meal.

INGREDIENTS

150g green beans, halved crosswise
6 boiled baby potatoes, halved or 1½ cups All-purpose Potatoes (see recipe page 70)
1 baby cos lettuce, chopped
1 cup cherry tomatoes, halved
2 x 185g tins best quality tuna in oil, drained
½ cup pitted Kalamata olives, quartered
2 tbsp capers (optional)
8 white anchovies (optional)
4 Tipsy Eggs (see recipe page 51), (see tip)

SALAD DRESSING

¼ cup extra virgin olive oil
2 tbsp red wine vinegar
1 garlic clove, minced or 1 tsp jarlic
salt n peppa's here
½ tsp Dijon mustard
½ tsp honey
squeeze lemon (optional)

To make the salad dressing, chuck all your ingredients in a small bowl and whisk, OR shake in a sealed glass jar, until emulsified.

Cook beans in a small saucepan of boiling water for 2 mins until just tender; drain and chuck into a bowl of iced water to stop the cooking process.

In a large salad bowl, gently combine all your salad ingredients EXCEPT the Tipsy Eggs. Cut eggs in half and arrange on top. Stick your salad in the fridge until you're ready to eat. Drizzle with salad dressing just before serving.

TIP If you don't have Tipsy Eggs already in the fridge, serve with with plain boiled eggs for a more traditional version. Bring a medium pan of water to the boil and drop eggs in gently. Cook at a rolling boil for 6½ mins for jammy eggs. Immediately transfer eggs to an ice bath to stop them cooking further.

Magician meals

PREP & COOK TIME 4 HRS 30 MINS SERVES 6

BASE RECIPE

Multi-Meat (Slow cooked beef & onion)

This rich beef and onion stew would be top of my list of dishes that I thought were vile as a child but now I LIVE off. I eat it on its own, on top of mash, in burritos, tacos, toasties, you name it. This is one of my weekly winners that can be eaten exactly as is, or served as the base for so many delicious off shoot meals, such as my Speedy Ragu and Cheesesteak Toastie on the following pages.

INGREDIENTS

1½ tbsp lotion (olive oil)
10g butter
1 large onion, thinly sliced
3 cloves garlic, minced or 3 tsp jarlic
1.5 kg chuck steak or casserole beef, trimmed of a little fat and cut into 4cm chunks
1½ tbsp tomato paste
1 tsp dried thyme, or a couple of sprigs of fresh thyme if you have it
2 bay leaves (optional)
1½ tbsp Who's Sister Sheree Sauce (Worcestershire sauce)
1½ cups chicken stock
1½ tbsp gravy granules or 1½ tbsp cornflour mixed with 1 tbsp water

If your multi cooker or slow cooker has a sauté function, turn it on; otherwise, heat a large casserole on a medium heat.

Put the lotion and butter in the cooker or dish. Add onion and garlic and cook for 3-4 mins until they're translucent. Cook your beef, in batches, searing on all sides until the meat starts to brown. Add the rest of the ingredients, EXCEPT for the gravy granules or cornflour slurry, and slow cook on LOW for 4-5 hours or on the stove, covered, on low heat, stirring occasionally for 3-4 hours.

Once your meat is tender, add the gravy granules or cornflour slurry mixture, and stir until sauce has thickened.

TIP Freeze Multi-Meat in airtight containers for up to 3 months.

MULTI-MEAT

Speedy Ragu

One of the myriad meals you can make with Multi-Meat is this super speedy ragu (that was a lot of alliteration, sorry). And it's about as simple as it gets.

PREP & COOK TIME 10 MINS SERVES 2

INGREDIENTS

1 cup Multi-Meat (see recipe page 56)

1 cup Saucy Minx Sauce (see recipe page 51)

200g fresh thick tagliatelle or pappardelle

finely grated parmesan and chopped green things (I like parsley), to serve

Combine your Multi-Meat and Saucy Minx Sauce in a small saucepan and stir well over medium heat for 5-6 mins. Cook until it's nice and hot.

Bring a large saucepan of water to the boil and cook your pasta according to packet instructions. Pour the sauce over your pasta and toss to combine.

Serve scattered with grated parmesan and chopped green things. And wine, obvs.

MULTI-MEAT

Cheesesteak Toastie

One of my life goals is to eat a genuine Philly Cheesesteak in Philadelphia. Preferably next to the giant statue of Rocky Balboa. Until such time as I can fulfill that wish, I'll eat these in my kitchen, singing Eye of the Tiger.

PREP & COOK TIME 15 MINS SERVES 2

INGREDIENTS

- **80g butter**
- **1 clove garlic, minced or 1 tsp jarlic**
- **4 large slices of fresh sourdough**
- **1½ cups Multi-Meat (see recipe page 56)**
- **4 slices of sharp nutty cheese (I like Swiss)**
- **¼ cup sliced pickled onions**

Combine butter and garlic, mix well and spread over both sides of each piece of bread.

Heat a large frying pan on medium heat. Lightly toast one side of each piece of bread in the pan until light golden. These will become the inside of each sandwich.

Heat your Multi-Meat in the microwave or in a small pan until warmed through. Spread on the toasted side of 2 slices of bread. Top with cheese, pickled onions and remaining bread toasted-side down.

Place sangas in the pan and cook for 5 mins each side until the cheese is melty and the bread is golden, garlicky and crunchy.

PREP & COOK TIME 30 MINS MAKES 10

MULTI-MEAT

Tac-achos

Why make Tacos or Nachos when you can make both at once? I don't understand the science behind this but these are SO much more delicious than tacos or nachos on their own. Ooey, gooey, crunchy, cheesy, savoury, messy, these are a doddle to make and a definite crowd pleaser.

INGREDIENTS

1 tbsp lotion (olive oil)
2 cups Multi-Meat (see recipe page 56)
½ x 30g packet taco seasoning
1 cup drained kidney beans
10 crunchy taco shells
1½ cups grated cheddar cheese
whatever taco toppings you love: chopped tomato, guacamole, sour cream, chopped coriander, pickled onion, sliced jalapeños or salsa, to serve

Heat a large frying pan on a medium heat. Put the lotion in the basket and add your Multi-Meat. Stir in your taco seasoning and kidney beans and fry this off for 5-8 mins until all the flavours are incorporated and meat is heated through.

Fill each taco shell with your seasoned meat and let it rain with cheese. Stand tacos up, in a baking dish (that will fit in your air fryer), side-by-side so they don't fall over. Add remaining Multi-Meat and cheese haphazardly all over the tacos like you would if you were making nachos. It should be messy!

Air fry at 180°C for 5-7 mins until the shells start to crisp and the cheese melts. Alternatively, cook in a preheated 200°C fan-forced oven for 8-10 mins.

Add your desired toppings all over your baked tacos making sure you get an even spread. You want each taco to be smothered and covered in toppings.

CONTORNI
You don't have to use Multi-Meat for this recipe. Your go-to taco meat or non meat will work just as well!

PREP & COOK TIME 50 MINS + MARINATING SERVES 4-6

BASE RECIPE

Utility Bird

This may well get me cancelled, but I'm not a huge fan of roast chicken. They're a b!tch to cook evenly, there's never enough seasoning and I'm not interested in eating the breast or wings. So I've done away with trying and I stick to what I know and love. The thigh. I'm a thigh guy through and through and this recipe is better than any whole roasted chook you've ever had.

INGREDIENTS

1.5kg bone in, skin on chicken thighs
1½ tbsp garlic powder
1½ tbsp onion powder
3 tsp smoked paprika
1½ tbsp lemon pepper seasoning
1½ tsp crack seasoning
salt n peppa's here
2 tbsp lotion (olive oil)

You can use a fancy meat thermometer if you have one, but I just take a thigh out once they look done and cut it open to see if its cooked through.

Preheat oven to 200°C fan-forced. Place a wire rack on a large oven tray.

Pat your chicken dry with paper towel to ensure they're as dry as possible. This helps the seasoning stick to the bird and ensure the crispiest skin. Set aside.

In a large bowl, chuck in all the spices, seasonings and salt n peppa and mix together. Add the chicken and a good glug of lotion and thoroughly toss well; you want every nook and cranny of the chicken covered in oil and seasoning. Stick in the fridge to marinate for 30 mins if you can.

Place your spiced chicken thighs on the rack and cook for 35-40 mins until golden and crisp and cooked through. The rack helps each entire piece of chook get crispy, not just the tops.

TIP Utility Bird is delicious served with a simple mashed sweet potato and steamed broccolini for a complete meal.

PREP & COOK TIME 15 MINS SERVES 4

UTILITY BIRD

Quick Chick Noodle Soup

If you're using a gorgeous home made chicken broth then you can probably skip the garlic, Italian herbs and crack seasoning. I've added them here assuming a lot of you will be making this with store-bought stock – which I do OFTEN!

INGREDIENTS

lotion (olive oil)
2 cloves garlic
½ tsp dried Italian herbs
½ cup chopped onion
½ cup chopped carrot
½ cup chopped celery
1.5 litres (6 cups) chicken stock
1 tsp crack seasoning
150g noodle of choice (I like angel hair pasta broken up)
2 cups chopped Utility Bird (see recipe page 63)
salt n peppa's here
chopped green things (I like parsley), to serve (optional)

Heat lotion in a large saucepan on medium heat. Chuck in your garlic, dried herbs, onion, carrot and celery. Sauté for 4 mins or until onion is translucent.

Add chicken stock and crack seasoning and bring to a gentle boil. Stir in your pasta and cook following the packet instructions.

Add the chopped Utility Bird and cook for a further 2 mins until warmed through. Season with salt n peppa.

Ladle soup into bowls. Serve scattered with chopped green things, if you wish.

TIP For a different spin, I sometimes add ginger, a splash of soy sauce, bok choy and a generous drizzle of chilli oil to make a "faux pho" soup. Add a Tipsy Egg (see recipe page 51) and Bob's your Uncle. Phenomenal.

PREP & COOK TIME 30 MINS MAKES 12

UTILITY BIRD

Nuggs

Legendary rapper Tupac once famously said: "I didn't choose the Nugg life, the Nugg life chose me." Okay, maybe he didn't say it exactly like that, but if you're the parent of a small child or even a large child, then you will know that nuggets ARE life. They are a life style, a life choice, and on many a harried week night, a life line. This super easy recipe is about as good as Nuggs get.

INGREDIENTS

- **2 cups finely chopped Utility Bird with the skin on (see recipe page 63)**
- **2 eggs, whisked**
- **¾ cup grated tasty cheddar cheese**
- **1 tbsp mayonnaise**
- **1 tsp cornflour**
- **1 tsp chicken salt or crack seasoning (optional)**
- **cooking spray**
- **tomato sauce, barbecue sauce or American mustard, to serve**

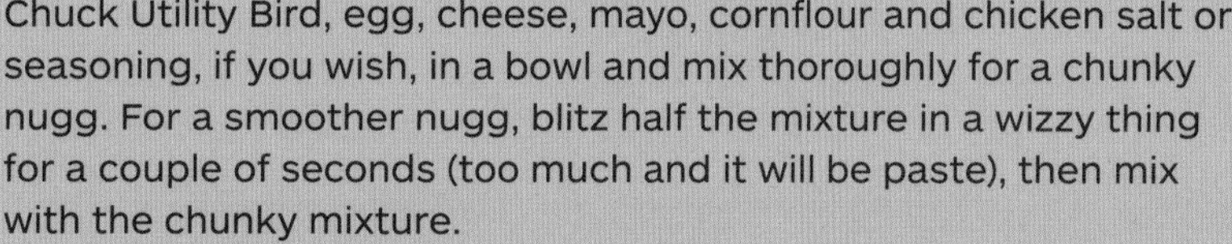

Chuck Utility Bird, egg, cheese, mayo, cornflour and chicken salt or seasoning, if you wish, in a bowl and mix thoroughly for a chunky nugg. For a smoother nugg, blitz half the mixture in a wizzy thing for a couple of seconds (too much and it will be paste), then mix with the chunky mixture.

Fashion heaped tablespoons of mixture into nugget shapes. Spritz them with oil spray for extra crunch if you desire (I usually do desire). Place in an air fryer basket and air fry at 180°C for 16-18 mins until golden and crispy. Alternatively, place on a wire rack on an oven tray and cook in a preheated 200°C fan-forced oven for 25-30 mins.

Serve Nuggs with your favourite sauce or mustard, if you wish.

TIP If you want to make a more ADULT VERSION of these nuggs (spoiler alert, you do), add chopped green things (I like chives), smoked paprika and chilli powder to your chicken mix. Correct. Top with taramasalata, sliced avocado and hand them out at your next swingers party.

PREP & COOK TIME 15 MINS SERVES 2 DRUNKARDS

UTILITY BIRD

Hangover Kebabs

This ultimate combination of flaky roti, fatty egg, salty chicken, carby chips, zingy tzatziki and punchy chilli oil will be sure to cure even the gnarliest of hangovers*.

** Hangover not required to enjoy this kebab.*

INGREDIENTS

2 tbsp lotion (olive oil)
2 frozen roti bread
2 eggs
1 cup sliced Utility Bird, skin on (see recipe page 63)
½ cup Tzatziki (see recipe page 51)
crispy chilli oil, to drizzle
handfuls of Frickles (see recipe page 27) (optional)
cooked frozen French fries, to serve (optional)

If you can't be bothered to make tzatziki, use your favourite store bought one.

Heat 1 tbsp of the lotion in a frying pan over medium heat. Cook each roti for 1-2 mins each side until flakey; transfer to a plate. Add the remaining lotion to same pan; crack in the eggs and fry for 3-4 mins. Transfer to same plate as roti.

Add Utility Bird to same hot pan and cook until heated through.

Top each roti bread with heated Utility Bird and a fried egg; spoon over tzatziki and drizzle with plenty of crispy chilli oil. Toss in a handful of Frickles if you fancy and wrap 'em up. Serve kebabs with French fries if your hangover needs them.

TIP Any leftover barbecue or roast chicken will work a treat here.

PREP & COOK TIME 55 MINS SERVES 6-8

BASE RECIPE

All-Purpose Potatoes

I love a roast potato, but I love a versatile potato even more. These All-Purpose Potatoes are neither completely boiled, nor completely roasted so it opens them up for re-modelling. As is, they're the perfect accompaniment to any meal, but feel free to transform the leftovers into any number of potato-y treats.

INGREDIENTS

2kg dirty potatoes, washed
1.5 litres (6 cups) chicken stock
1/3 cup lotion (olive oil)
4 garlic cloves, minced or 2 tsp jarlic
1 lemon, finely grated zest and juice
1 tsp crack seasoning
1 tsp salt (optional or to taste)
½ cup chopped green things (I like parsley and mint)

Preheat oven to 200°C fan-forced. Line a large roasting pan or baking dish with baking paper.

Peel your potatoes and cut them in half or quarters, if large. Pour chicken stock into a large saucepan then add 2 cups water and bring to a gentle boil.

Add your potatoes to the pan and top up with extra water, if you think it needs it to fully cover the potatoes. Simmer for around 10 mins until the potatoes are tender, but not breaking apart. Drain well and transfer to the lined roasting pan. You may need to spread them across two pans.

To the potatoes, add the lotion, garlic, lemon zest and juice, crack seasoning and salt. Toss gently to coat well. Cook in the oven for 15 mins until slightly golden. We're not roasting the potatoes here, just crispifying them slightly for the other recipes. If you want to eat them now, continue roasting for another 15 mins until golden and crispy. Make it rain with chopped green things.

ALL-PURPOSE POTATOES

Easiest Veggie Curry

Carbs on carbs is my idea of a perfect meal. And since I'm a glutton for punishment, I serve this carb on carb curry on a bed of rice with a side of roti. Quadruple the carbs, quadruple the happiness.

PREP & COOK TIME 30 MINS SERVES 2

INGREDIENTS

2 tbsp ghee
1 onion, diced
2 tbsp curry powder
400g can chickpeas, drained and rinsed
¼ batch All-Purpose Potatoes, chopped (see recipe page 70)
2 cups Saucy Minx Sauce (see recipe page 51) or 2 cups canned diced tomatoes
¼ cup cream (optional)
steamed basmati rice, roti and green things (I like coriander), to serve

Heat a large frying pan on medium heat, add your ghee and sauté onion for 5 mins until translucent. Add curry powder and fry off for 2 mins until fragrant. Add chickpeas and potatoes then thoroughly coat them in the spices.

Add your Saucy Minx Sauce (or canned tomatoes), bubble away on LOW heat for 15 mins (or longer if you have the time and/or the patience). Stir in your cream, if you wish.

Serve curry with basmati rice and roti, then make it rain with green things.

ALL-PURPOSE POTATOES

Home Fries

I fell in love with these American pan-roasted breakfast potatoes while living there. They're good with anything, anytime – and for me, that craving hits daily.

PREP & COOK TIME 20 MINS SERVES 2

INGREDIENTS

1 tbsp lotion (olive oil)
½ onion, finely diced
20g butter
¼ batch All-Purpose Potatoes (see recipe page 70), cut into smaller chunks
½ tsp garlic powder
½ tsp smoked paprika
salt n peppa's here
bacon, fried eggs and chives, to serve (optional)

Heat 2 tsp lotion in a large frying pan on medium heat. Sauté your onion for 5 mins until translucent and starting to brown. Remove from pan and set aside.

Add remaining lotion and butter to same pan. Chuck in your All-Purpose Potatoes and fry for 5-6 mins, turning occasionally or until light golden. The trick is to not stir too much. Toss in your spices and salt n peppa and return the onions to the pan, gently combine. Fry for a further 2-3 mins until everything is golden, crispy and smelling ridiculously good.

For super-duper crispy potatoes, you can stick them under a hot grill for a few minutes. Serve immediately with bacon, fried eggs, and chopped chives, if you desire.

PREP & COOK TIME 20 MINS SERVES 2

ALL-PURPOSE POTATOES

Jacket Potato & Leek Soup

What to do if you feel like a jacket potato but don't feel like chewing? You make this soup is what you do. I actually prefer this to a baked potato. It has way more flavour and you can batch make it for an endless supply in the freezer.

INGREDIENTS

2 tbsp lotion (olive oil), plus extra to drizzle (optional)
1 cup chopped leek
2 cloves garlic, minced or 2 tsp jarlic
¼ batch All-Purpose Potatoes (see recipe page 70)
3 cups chicken or veg stock, approximately
½ tsp crack seasoning (optional)
3 rashers bacon, rind removed
⅓ cup thickened cream
salt n peppa's here
sour cream, chopped green things (I like chives) and cheesy toasts, to serve

Sprinkle the soup with my Cheesy Garlic Crouton Crumble (see recipe page 51), if you wish (and you do!).

Heat a large saucepan on a medium heat. Put the lotion in the basket, add your leek and garlic and sauté for 5 mins until the leek is soft and fragrant and ever so slightly browning. Add your potatoes and continue to fry for 2-3 mins.

Add stock and crack seasoning, if using. Let this bubble away for about 5 mins by which time the leek should be completely cooked.

While the soup is simmering, heat a medium frying pan over medium-high heat and fry your bacon until caramelised and beginning to crisp. Roughly chop and set aside.

Use a stick blender or whizzy thing to blend your soup until smooth, return to the pan; stir through the cream and extra stock if you want a thinner soup. Add salt n peppa, stir until heated through.

Ladle soup into bowls. Dollop with sour cream, then scatter with chopped bacon, green things and more peppa. Drizzle with a little extra lotion, if desired. Serve with cheesy toasts.

Afternoon delight

PREP & COOK TIME 20 MINS + FREEZING MAKES 16 PIECES

Better-than-a-Snickers Slice

I don't call this "Better-than-a-Snickers" lightly. Snickers are my favourite chocolate bar, but this slice feels so boujee and elevated; I honestly prefer it. And yes, I think it's healthier too, which makes eating five times as much totally justifiable.

INGREDIENTS

16 medjool dates, pitted
½ cup smooth peanut butter (see tip)
½ cup chopped nuts (I like walnuts or pecans)
180g dark chocolate, broken into pieces
2 tsp coconut oil
good pinch salt flakes

Place dates, cut-side down, side-by-side on a lined oven tray and squish them with your hands to form a rough square. Pour the peanut butter evenly over the squashed dates and sprinkle with nuts.

Melt chocolate and coconut oil in a microwave-safe bowl, in the microwave on high for 30-45 seconds; stir until melted. Pour evenly over the nuts and sprinkle with a good pinch of salt flakes.

Freeze slice for 20 mins until firm. Cut into squares. Store in the freezer for best results.

TIP If your peanut butter isn't runny, pop it in the microwave for about 20 seconds.

PREP & COOK TIME 25 MINS MAKES 16

Lemonade Scones

Ever since I was introduced to Bojana's buns, I've been obsessed with quick, few ingredient recipes. This nails the brief. Prepped and cooked within 30 mins, these scones are heavenly with lashings of jam and whipped cream, just butter, or as the base for any sweet-flavoured scone you love.

INGREDIENTS

3 cups self-raising flour
¾ cup chilled lemonade
300ml thickened cream
raspberry jam and whipped cream, to serve

In a large mixing bowl, add your flour. Pour in your lemonade and cream and mix until well combined.

Roll or press out the dough on a lightly floured surface into a round until 3cm thick. Using a floured 6cm scone cutter, cut dough into rounds. Re-roll any offcuts and cut our more rounds.

Place scones in the air fryer basket or on a baking-paper-lined oven tray, leaving room between each scone for expansion.

Air fry at 180°C for 10 mins, then flip them over and cook for another 2-3 mins until light golden. Alternatively, bake in a preheated 180°C fan-forced oven for 15 mins or until golden. You can always flip and cook for longer if you like.

Serves warm scones with jam and cream.

TIPS I often turn this mix into date scones (just add 1 cup of chopped dates). If you have any leftover scones, use these in the Scone & Butter Pudding (see recipe page 122).

PREP & COOK TIME 15 MINS (+ FREEZING) MAKES 10 SLICES

Cranberry Ripe

This recipe was my first viral video on socials, and it sums up my cooking style: use what you have, measure with your heart, bung it together, add salt and hope for the best.

INGREDIENTS

1 cup dried sweetened cranberries
3 medjool dates, pitted and coarsely chopped
1 cup MOIST coconut flakes (see tip)
¼ tsp vanilla extract
180g chocolate, broken into pieces (I like a mix of dark and milk)
2 tsp coconut oil
a good pinch salt flakes

Line base and sides of a 10cm x 20cm loaf pan with baking paper.

In a food processor, blitz your cranberries, dates, coconut and vanilla for a few seconds until fruit has minced together.

Melt chocolate and coconut oil in a microwave-safe bowl, in the microwave on high for 30-45 seconds; stir until melted. Drizzle half your chocolate mixture over the bottom of the loaf pan, smooth it out. Freeze for 15 mins until firm.

Spread cranberry mixture evenly over the chocolate, using your fingers to press down gently. Pour remaining chocolate mixture over the top, then smooth it out with the back of a spoon. If the remaining chocolate mixture has started to set while waiting on the bench, just re-melt it in the microwave for about 20 seconds or until it's pourable again. Sprinkle with a pinch of salt flakes. Freeze for 20 minutes until firm. Cut into about 10 slices. Store slices in the freezer for best results. (And to hide them from the rest of your family.)

TIP Moist Coconut Flakes are preferable to regular desiccated coconut. If you can't find them, mix desiccated coconut with ½ tsp sugar and 1 tsp milk.

PIMP MY BOX

CARTON CAKE, 2 WAYS

Lemon Coconut Cake

PREP & COOK TIME 45 MINS
SERVES 8

Grease and line a 20cm round cake pan. Use 1 x 450g-470g vanilla cake mix with icing. Follow box instructions using ingredients listed on the box to make your cake mix. Finely grate zest of 1 lemon and juice the lemon, add ¾ of both the zest and juice to the batter with 1 cup MOIST coconut flakes. Pour batter into prepared pan and bake following box instructions. Cool completely. Toast ¼ cup MOIST coconut flakes in a frying pan over low heat for 2-3 mins stirring until golden. Follow box instructions using ingredients listed to make the icing; add remaining lemon zest and juice and stir well. Spread icing over cake and scatter with cooled toasted coconut and extra finely grated lemon zest, if you like.

Cheat's Berry Sponge

PREP & COOK TIME 50 MINS
SERVES 8

Grease and line a 20cm round cake pan. Use 1 x 450g-470g vanilla cake mix with icing; reserve the icing for another use. Follow box instructions using ingredients listed on the box to make your cake mix. Pour batter into prepared pan and bake following box instructions. Cool completely. Split cake in half horizontally (like a layer cake). Whip 300ml thickened cream until firm peaks form. Spread ½ cup jam onto the top of the bottom cake layer. Spread half the cream over the jam and replace with the top layer of cake. Spread remaining cream over top of cake and decorate with quartered or halved strawberries.

PREP & COOK TIME 35 MINS MAKES 8

Stinky Bums

The first time I made these for my son, I asked him if he'd like a sticky bun. He replied "Yes, I do like a stinky bum." So they will naturally be known hence as Stinky Bums. And who doesn't want a warm, stinky bum in their mouth?

INGREDIENTS

½ portion of Lemonade Scone dough (see recipe page 81)
extra flour for rolling
2 tbsp caster sugar
1½ tsp ground cinnamon
40g butter, melted

GLAZE

½ cup icing sugar mixture
¼ tsp vanilla extract (if you have it)
2 tbsp milk, approximately

You can add 2 hefty tbsp cream cheese and a hefty tbsp butter to the glaze ingredients to make a cream cheese frosting. My personal kryptonite.

Preheat oven to 200°C fan-forced. Line an oven tray with baking paper.

On a lightly floured surface, roll the scone dough into a rough rectangle 20cm x 32cm. You may need to add extra flour if your dough is very sticky.

In a small bowl, combine your sugar, cinnamon and melted butter. Brush cinnamon butter evenly over your scone dough. Roll up from the long side (so you get a long, thin log as opposed to a short, fat one). Cut into 8 slices roughly 4cm thick.

Place scone scrolls on the lined tray, next to each other so they are just touching. Bake for 15 mins or until golden. Cool slightly.

To make your glaze, sift icing sugar into a bowl. Add vanilla and 1½ tbsp of the milk and mix until smooth; add the rest of the milk if needed to make it drizzly.

Drizzle the glaze over your still-warm scrolls so it slightly melts into them.

CHEF

PREP & COOK TIME 1 HR + COOLING SERVES 10

A.I. (Orange) Cake

One day my son requested his Dad make him an orange cake. Being a tech nerd to his core, Dad bypassed the litany of cookbooks on our shelves and consulted ChatGPT instead. The result being the most perfect orange cake I've ever eaten.

Also, I did my due diligence and asked for the original source of this recipe to give credit, but apparently it's a ChatGPT original so I'm not stealing from anyone (except maybe Bill Gates, which I'm ok with).

INGREDIENTS

125g soft unsalted butter
1 cup caster sugar
2 eggs
finely grated zest of 2 oranges
½ cup freshly squeezed orange juice
¼ cup milk
1 tsp vanilla extract
1½ cups self-raising flour
½ tsp bicarbonate of soda

ORANGE GLAZE

½ cup icing sugar mixture
2 tbsp fresh orange juice, approx

Preheat the oven to 180°C fan-forced. Grease and line a 10cm x 20cm loaf pan.

In a medium bowl, cream butter and sugar together. You can go hell for leather by hand or use an electric mixer. Add your eggs, one by one, making sure to mix well after each addition. Mix in the orange zest, juice, milk and vanilla until combined.

Sift flour, bicarb and a pinch of salt over the wet ingredients, then gently mix through.

Pour mixture into prepared pan and bake for about 35 mins or until a skewer comes out clean. Cover cake loosely with foil if it's browning too quickly in the oven. Cool completely.

To make the orange glaze, mix icing sugar with enough orange juice to make a pourable icing, that's nice and smooth.

Drizzle or spread the glaze over your cooled cake before cutting into slices to serve.

LG
CHILLI

2020
CRISPY
CHILLI OIL

PIMP MY BOX

BOX BROWNIE, 2 WAYS

Banana Pecan Brownie Bites

PREP & COOK TIME 45 MINS
MAKES 16

Grease and line a 20cm square cake pan. Use 1 x 560g-580g box brownie mix with icing. Follow box instructions using ingredients listed on the box to make your brownie batter. Add in 1 mashed devil spawn banana and mix well. Add your ⅔ cup chopped pecans. Spoon batter into prepared pan and bake following box instructions. Cool brownies completely. Make icing following box instructions; spread over cooled brownie and scatter with extra chopped pecans. Cut into 16 squares.

Cheesecake Brookies

PREP & COOK TIME 40 MINS
MAKES 12

Grease a 12-hole (⅓ cup/80ml) muffin pan with cooking oil spray. Use 1 x 500g box triple choc fudge brownie mix without icing. Follow box instructions using ingredients listed on the box to make your brownie batter. In the bowl of an electric mixer, mix 225g cream cheese with 1 egg, ¼ cup caster sugar and ½ tsp vanilla extract until fluffy. Pour the brownie mix halfway into each muffin hole. Pour the cheesecake mix on top of the brownie mix until almost to the top. You can bake like this OR using a skewer, swirl the brownie and cheesecake mix together. Bake 25-30 mins until almost firm to touch. Cool in pan before transferring to a wire rack.

Death row dinners

No-groan-i

PREP TIME 5 MINS SERVES 1

INGREDIENTS

30ml gin of choice
30ml Campari
30ml sweet vermouth
handful of ice
1 sprig rosemary
slice of orange rind, to garnish

I've been known to use dry vermouth to save me buying another bottle, but sweet is best.

Add all your ingredients to a cocktail shaker EXCEPT the rosemary and orange rind, then shake it like a polaroid picture. Technically you're meant to stir Negronis but I always shake. You do you.

Pour into your glass with or without the ice.

Grab a lighter and run it across your rosemary sprig a few times to toast it slightly and release the oils and aroma. Stir your cocktail with the torched sprig and pat yourself on the back for being so posh. Garnish with the orange rind to make it even fancier.

Filthy Martini

PREP TIME 5 MINS SERVES 2

INGREDIENTS

4 fat green olives, pip in
2 toothpicks
120ml your choice of gin
20ml dry vermouth
40-60ml olive brine, the murkier the better
large handful of ice
a few drops of olive oil

Place 2 olives on each toothpick.

Fill your large cocktail shaker with remaining ingredients EXCEPT the oil. Shake it like a polaroid picture.

Strain into 2 icy cold martini glasses. Add a few drops of olive oil and your olive skewer to each.

Congratulations, you just made the greatest cocktail on earth.

SCAN TO SEE IN ACTION!

Yuzu Fizz

PREP TIME 5 MINS   SERVES 1

INGREDIENTS

45ml gin of choice
30ml yuzu juice (or a mix of lemon and lime juice)
15ml simple syrup (1:1 water to sugar)
1 egg white
handful of ice
chilled soda water, to top up
thin strip lemon rind, to garnish

Chuck all ingredients into your cocktail shaker EXCEPT soda water and garnish, and shake it like a polaroid picture for around 20 seconds until frothy. Technically you're supposed to shake WITHOUT ice for maximum frothage, and then WITH ice but I can never be bothered with this step.

Strain into your glass, leaving the ice behind. Top up with a dash of soda water and garnish with your lemon rind. Look how fancy you are!

Like a vir-GIN

PREP TIME 5 MINS SERVES 1

INGREDIENTS

60ml gin of choice
30ml St Germain
20ml lime juice
30ml cranberry juice
1 dash orange bitters
handful of ice
chilled Prosecco, to top up
a sprig of mint and a slice of lime, to garnish

Add all ingredients EXCEPT Prosecco and garnishes to a cocktail shaker and shake it like a polaroid picture.

Strain into your glass, leaving the ice behind. Top up with Prosecco and garnish with a sprig of mint and a slice of lime.

PREP & COOK TIME 15 MINS SERVES 4

Bruschetta Bites

My Mum used to make me bruschetta as a child as a treat. It felt like such a fancy bite to be consuming outside of a restaurant. It wasn't until semi adulthood that I realised just how simple these are to make. You've probably got all the ingredients in your kitchen right now – what are you waiting for?

INGREDIENTS

1 punnet sweet cherry tomatoes, coarsely chopped
1 tbsp finely chopped green things (I like basil)
1 tbsp balsamic vinegar, plus extra for drizzling
salt n peppa's here
1 good-quality baguette
2 cloves garlic, minced or 2 tsp jarlic
¼ cup lotion (olive oil), plus extra for drizzling

Preheat oven to 200°C fan-forced and lightly oil an oven tray.

Chuck your cherry tomatoes, green things, balsamic and salt n peppa to taste in a bowl. Give it a gentle stir and set aside.

Cut your baguette diagonally into 2cm thick slices. Add your garlic to the lotion and brush over baguette slices; pop them on the oiled tray. Bake for about 5 mins or until the baguette slices are looking golden and crunchy.

Remove your toasted baguette slices from the oven and top with your marinated tomato mixture. Drizzle each bruschetta bite with an extra drop of balsamic and a little extra oil. Consume immediately!

PREP & COOK TIME 15 MINS SERVES 4

Saucy Minx Prawn Spaghettini

If you ask me, this is the Meryl Streep of pastas. The undisputed GOAT. The sweetness of the prawns and sauce, the chew of the pasta, the punch of heat from the chilli oil? Perfection. If a gigantic bowl of this was served to me as my last meal on earth, I'd die a happy death. Note: don't listen to haters who say parmesan doesn't belong on seafood. You can and should bury this dish under a mountain of cheese.

INGREDIENTS

2 tbsp lotion (olive oil)
1-2 small fresh red chillies, deseeded and chopped
300g raw peeled and deveined prawns with tails intact
3 cups Saucy Minx Sauce (see recipe page 51)
400g spaghettini
loads of grated parmesan, cracked peppa, chopped green things (I like basil) and chilli oil, to serve

Heat the lotion in a large frying pan on a medium-high heat. Add chopped chilli and your prawns and sauté for 2 mins turning prawns over. Add Saucy Minx Sauce and simmer for 2 mins until prawns are just cooked.

Meanwhile, cook the spaghettini in a large saucepan of boiling water following packet instructions. Drain and return to the pan. Add your sauce to the cooked pasta and toss to coat well.

Serve saucy pasta scattered with parmesan, peppa and green things, then drizzle with chilli oil.

PREP & COOK TIME 1 HR SERVES 4

World's Easiest Apple Crumble Tart

As much as I love to eat a traditional apple pie, I hate to make it. Pastry from scratch, blind baking, faffing around with the crust? No thanks. I just want hot sweet apples and pastry in my mouth without the rigmarole. This recipe delivers on both counts.

INGREDIENTS

1¼ ready-made frozen puff pastry sheets
1½ tbsp warmed jam (I like apricot)
1½ Granny Smith apples, quartered, cored, thickly sliced
20g butter, softened
1 tbsp caster sugar
½ tsp ground cinnamon
1 tbsp milk
vanilla ice-cream, to serve

CRUMBLE TOPPING

½ cup plain flour
⅓ cup caster sugar
80g butter, softened

This really is the world's easiest crumble, and it can be used to pimp up literally any muffin, cake, pie or banana bread you make.

Preheat oven to 200°C fan-forced, with an oven tray inside to get hot.

For the crumble topping, chuck everything into a bowl and mix until combined. Store in the fridge or freezer until ready to use. Makes around 1 cup.

Place your still frozen whole pastry sheet on a piece of baking paper. Using your extra pastry piece, cut four 2cm-ish wide strips and place one on each edge of pastry sheet to form a border. You want the edges to have a double layer of pastry. Reserve remaining pastry for another use.

Spread 1 tbsp jam over the pastry, leaving the border jam free.

In a medium bowl, add apple slices, butter, sugar and cinnamon. Massage together until the apples are smothered in the buttery, sugary, cinnamony mix.

Artfully (or not) place your apple slices on top of the jam until your pastry is covered. I like to overlap them slightly, but you do you!

In the same bowl you used for the apples and sugar, whisk together the remaining jam and the milk. I'm lazy and use a pastry brush for this. Using the pastry brush, coat the edges of your pastry with jam mixture, and use it to glaze the apples too.

Crumble or grate ¼ cup of cold crumble topping over the apples. Reserve remaining crumble for another use.

Pick up the baking paper with your tart on board and CAREFULLY place directly onto the HOT oven tray in the oven. Bake for 30 mins or until the apples begin to caramelise and pastry is puffed and golden. Serve with vanilla ice-cream.

AMORE

Uncle Trent The Wrangler

Always tired

Forced cuddles

Bowie & Bruno, my rescue babies

Working on his man-spread

A restful nap with Daddio

Two world-class cuddlers

The price of dating a tall man

Heaven

Who's not a morning person?

Never happier #hotwheels

PREP & COOK TIME 50 MINS + MARINATING SERVES 4

Hyperfixation Noodles

I'm not going to lie, this recipe is what I call "a faff around". Not my usual M.O. BUT. Oh my word. You will become addicted. Be warned. I used to order this on Uber Eats multiple times a week until I realised I could save time and money if I just made it at home. I batch make all the elements of this recipe and store them in the fridge so I can toss them together whenever the need arises. Which is very often, FYI.

INGREDIENTS

500g pork belly rashers, rind removed, cut into 3cm pieces
2 tbsp peanut oil (or any mild oil)
8 store-bought frozen spring rolls
200g vermicelli noodles
1 cup Frickles (see recipe page 27)
¼ iceberg lettuce, shredded
1 large carrot, shredded
1 cup torn fresh basil and mint leaves
½ cup crushed peanuts
1 long red chilli, thinly sliced

MARINADE

2 tbsp fish sauce
2 tbsp light soy sauce
1 tbsp brown sugar
1 tbsp honey
1 tbsp peanut oil (or any mild oil)
1 tsp sesame oil
3 cloves garlic, minced
½ red onion or 2 shallots, thinly sliced
1 stalk lemongrass, smashed (see tips)

DRESSING

2 tbsp fish sauce
¼ cup lime juice
1½ tbsp caster sugar
2 garlic cloves, minced
1 bird's eye chilli, finely chopped (see tips)

For the marinade, chuck all the ingredients in a large airtight container and shake well to combine.

Chuck pork into the marinade, and shake vigorously to coat pork in marinade. Stick in the fridge for a few hours or overnight.

Heat peanut oil in a large pan or wok on medium-high heat. When the pan is super hot, fry your pork and marinade, in batches, for 5-6 mins until golden. Return all the pork to the pan and cook until glazed and sticky. This can burn easily, so keep an eagle eye and lower heat if necessary. Set aside.

Cook spring rolls and the vermicelli noodles following their packet instructions.

For the dressing, place all the ingredients in a jar with ¼ cup water and shake vigorously.

Divide the noodles among your bowls; top with sticky pork, Frickles, lettuce, carrot, spring rolls, herbs, peanuts and chilli. Drown your salad in the dressing and devour.

TIPS Deseed the chilli, before chopping if you don't like your head being blown off. Using lemongrass in the marinade is optional, but I highly recommend that you do.

PREP TIME 15 MINS SERVES 4

Viral Cuke Salad

Viral for good reason. This salad is out of this world delicious, easy to make and stays good in the fridge for a couple of days. Actually, I can't vouch for that, because I always eat the entire portion immediately. In theory it should stay good for a couple days in the fridge.

INGREDIENTS

3 Lebanese cucumbers, ends trimmed
1 tsp fine salt
2 cloves garlic, minced
1 tbsp light soy sauce
1 tbsp rice vinegar
2 tsp black vinegar
1 tsp caster sugar
2 tbsp crispy chilli oil
1 tsp sesame oil
¼ tsp crack seasoning or msg (optional)
1 tbsp toasted sesame seeds, for sprinkling

With a rolling pin or the base of a heavy glass, lightly smash the cucumbers so they break apart slightly. Cut into bite-sized chunks, then chuck into a glass jar or bowl and sprinkle with salt. Leave for 10 mins so any excess water drains from the cukes.

Discard the excess water from the jar or bowl. Add all remaining ingredients EXCEPT the sesame seeds. Seal your glass jar and shake it like a polaroid picture. You want all the ingredients mixed thoroughly.

When you're ready to serve, transfer your cukes to a serving bowl, sprinkle over your sesame seeds and try to refrain from salivating all over the place.

PREP & COOK TIME 30 MINS + FREEZING MAKES 6

Fried Ice-Cream

I don't usually go in for ANYTHING high maintenance. But sometimes, as is the case with this recipe, it's worth it. These are actually super simple to make, it's just the re-dipping and re-freezing element that as a deeply impatient person I find intolerable. But these fried ice-cream balls are so impressive, I will go the extra mile. They're that good.

INGREDIENTS

150g digestive biscuits
1 egg
2 tbsp runny honey
1 litre vanilla ice-cream
cooking oil spray
sliced fresh mango, to serve

Coated ice-cream balls can be stored in the freezer, for up to 1 week, ready to cook and indulge in at a moment's notice.

Place a baking-paper-lined oven tray in the freezer for 10 mins.

Place digestive biscuits in a sealed ziplock bag and bash with a rolling pin until you have a fine crumb or chuck them in a food processor and whizz until fine crumbs form. It should look like sand. Pour into a medium-sized bowl.

Whisk your egg and honey in another medium-sized bowl

Scoop out hefty balls of ice-cream, about the size of a small orange. Place on the chilled lined oven tray and return to the freezer.

Toss the frozen ice-cream balls, one at a time in the biscuit crumb until well coated. You can use your hands for this if you're quick. Dip your crumbed ice-cream in your eggy honey bath until well coated. Re-toss in the biscuit crumbs until you have a thick coating around your ice-cream. Place them back on the lined tray.

Stick them back in the freezer for at least 2 hours.

When your coated ice-cream balls are frozen solid, lightly spritz with cooking spray and air fry at 200°C for 3 mins. I like to fry my balls separately to ensure a crisp crust with no meltage.

Serve with fresh sliced mango.

Lazy Caprezy

Drown a toasted slice of focaccia or any bread you have (carbs are an essential food group) with 2-3 tbsp pesto. Top with 1 sliced tomato and 2 sliced bocconcini. Season with lots of peppa and scatter with fresh torn basil leaves. Drizzle with some lotion (olive oil).

READY IN: MINUTES SERVES: 1 HANGRY MUM CALORIES: WHO CARES?

MUM'S DINNER

Deli in My Belly

Chuck a few slices of your favourite deli meats on a plate or platter (I like prosciutto, salami, bresaola, Danish salami, and fennel & garlic salami) with a couple of wedges of cheese (I like provolone or blue cheese, but use whatever you have). Drown it all in Thousand Island dressing.

NOTE: 1-2 GLASSES OF WINE IS RECOMMENDED WITH EACH OF THESE MEALS, TO AID DIGESTION. BUT DON'T DRINK STRAIGHT FROM THE BOTTLE, YOU'RE BETTER THAN THAT.

Jap in a Snap

Mix a 95g can drained tuna with 1-2 tbsp sriracha mayo. Spoon this over 1 cup warmed Recycle Rice (see recipe page 34) or 1 packet heated microwave rice, and top with ½ sliced avocado. Drizzle with crispy chilli oil and make it rain with crushed nori or sesame seeds if you're fancy.

Chippety Dippety Doo

Place dip of choice, store bought or any leftover Tzatziki (see recipe page 51) on a plate. Add a large quantity of crisps (plain salted for me, but you do you), some sliced cheddar cheese and a sliced apple (for health).

TIP No prep is required here. I highly recommend eating straight from the fridge/tub/packet. But use a glass for the wine.

PREP TIME 10 MINS SERVES 4

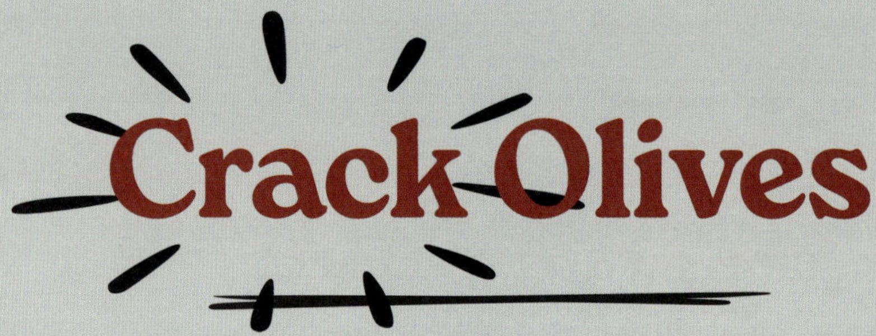

Crack Olives

You know you've crossed the Rubicon into adulthood when you retire the Salt and Vinegar chips and instead put a bowl of olives out to impress your friends. Happy to be growing old if these crack olives are involved.

INGREDIENTS

1 cup Sicilian Green olives
1 cup Kalamata olives
1 tbsp olive brine
¾ cup olive oil
1 long red chilli, thinly sliced
3 cloves garlic, thinly sliced
1 tsp dried oregano
2 sprigs fresh thyme or ½ tsp dried thyme
rind of 1 lemon, cut in 2cm strips
crackers and cheese, to serve

If you can't be bothered to slice the garlic, just crush it.

Bung everything into a glass jar or glass container and that's it!

Leave the jar in the fridge to marinate for as long as you can. The longer the better.

Remove olives from the fridge 1 hour before serving, they are even better eaten at room temperature.

Serve with crackers and cheese.

CAPITAL
BREWING CO
COAST

PREP & COOK TIME 30 MINS SERVES 4

Crispy Fat Fish & Fancy Salad

This dish reminds me of being in my 20s and actually having the time and wish to cook pretty meals. Also, back then I happily lived next to a glorious Italian supermarket that introduced me to fancy things like witlof and fennel. Good times!

INGREDIENTS

4 x 180g fillets fatty salmon, skin on
1 tbsp lotion (olive oil)
salt n peppa's here

FANCY SALAD

1 large orange
1 witlof, leaves separated
1 small raddicchio, leaves torn
1 bulb fennel, thinly sliced
75g drained marinated goat's cheese or Persian feta
2 tbsp coarsely chopped green things (I like dill)

DRESSING

1/3 cup oil
1½ tbsp red wine vinegar
½ tsp Dijon mustard

If you're a certified MENSA genius and can pan fry salmon without burning it then forget the air fryer and go ahead and just do that. Show off.

To make the fancy salad, slice the rind and pith off your orange so just the juicy fleshy, naked orange remains. Thinly slice into segments. Catch any juice in a bowl and save it for the dressing; you will need 1½ tbsp juice.

Arrange witlof leaves, radicchio, sliced orange and fennel on a platter, crumble over your goat's cheese or feta and scatter over your dill. Set salad aside while you do the dressing and fish.

To make the dressing, chuck everything into a jar; add reserved orange juice from salad, seal the top and shake it like a polaroid picture until emulsified.

Pat your salmon dry with paper towel, then toss in a small bowl with the lotion and a pinch of salt n peppa. Make sure that the skin of the salmon is especially well coated in oil and seasoning. I usually add a bit more oil, salt and peppa to the skin for maximum crispiness.

Heat a large frying pan on a medium-high heat, sear the salmon SKIN SIDE DOWN for 1-2 mins until there is nice colour and crisp to the salmon skin.

Transfer the salmon to an air fryer basket SKIN SIDE DOWN. Air fry at 180°C for 7-10 mins depending on how thick the fillets are. Alternatively, put the salmon on an oven tray and stick it in a preheated 180°C fan-forced oven for 11-14 mins. I like my salmon quite soft, but feel free to cook for longer if you like it well done.

Cover your salad with the dressing and serve beside crispy fat fish.

PREP & COOK TIME 40 MINS SERVES 4

Scone & Butter Pudding

I love making scones. They're quick and easy and go down a treat when served fresh from the oven. However, the difference between a perfect, fluffy, soft scone and an inedible rock is about half a day so I often have uneaten, stale scones lying around the house. Hence, Scone & Butter Pudding. This is recycling at its finest so you need not feel any guilt consuming this pud. It would be wrong not to.

INGREDIENTS

10 stale scones (I like to use date scones for this)
120g butter, softened
3 eggs
1½ cups milk
225ml thickened cream
1 tsp vanilla extract
⅓ cup caster sugar, plus extra for sprinkling
sprinkle of ground cinnamon
ice-cream and maple syrup, to serve

Preheat your oven to 180°C fan-forced.

Cut your scones in half and butter each side. Once buttered, cut again into generous chunks and arrange in a 2-litre (8-cup) capacity, 18cm x 24cm baking dish.

To make the custard, in a medium-sized bowl, whisk your eggs, milk, cream, vanilla, sugar and cinnamon. Pour your custard mix over your chopped scones making sure the scones are evenly drenched. Sprinkle an extra teaspoon of sugar evenly over the top.

Bake pudding for 30 mins or until the custard has set and the tips of the scones are golden. Serve with scoops of ice-cream and drizzle with maple syrup.

TIP This will work with almost any uneaten cake, muffin, banana bread you have laying around. I freeze my uneaten baked goods and pull them out when I have enough to make this pudding.

Glossary

If some of the terminology in this book doesn't make sense, it's because it doesn't. Here's a cheat's guide to understanding my kitchen language:

CLARICE My multi cooker which I use as a slow cooker most of the time (I highly recommend naming your kitchen gadgets if you haven't already).

STEVEN My air fryer; one of my favourite kitchen friends.

THE LOTION Olive oil or extra virgin olive oil, add it to your pan/bowl liberally.

CRACK SEASONING Chicken (or veg) stock powder to boost flavour.

SALT N PEPPA'S HERE Season with salt and pepper to taste.

WHIZZY THING Any kitchen appliance that blitzes your mixture into a puree or paste.

PIMP IT Enhance an already tasty thing with more tasty things.

JARLIC Minced garlic from a jar.

GINJAR Minced ginger from a jar.

MAKE IT RAIN Sprinkle the ingredients enthusiastically as if you were throwing dollar bills.

GREEN THINGS Optional fresh herb adornments such as parsley, chives and coriander.

DEVIL SPAWN BANANA A banana so ripe it looks as if it were birthed by Satan.

CORRECT Yum and/or delicious.

For Example

Switch on Clarice, and put the lotion in the basket. Add your meat and crack seasoning. Salt n peppa's here. Blitz your veg in the whizzy thing and add to Clarice. Pimp it by adding some Jarlic. When it's done, make it rain with green things. Correct.

Translation

Turn on your multi cooker to slow cook and pour in oil. Add your meat, stock powder, salt and pepper. Add your blended veggies. Garlic would work well here. Once cooked, sprinkle with parsley and you're done. Delicious.

Conversion chart

MEASURES

One Australian metric measuring cup holds approximately 250ml; one Australian metric tablespoon holds 20ml; one Australian metric teaspoon holds 5ml. The difference between one country's measuring cups and another's is within a two- or three-teaspoon variance and will not affect your cooking results. North America, New Zealand and the United Kingdom use a 15ml tablespoon. All cup and spoon measurements are level.

When measuring liquids, use a clear glass or plastic jug with the metric markings.

We use extra-large eggs with an average weight of 60g each.

DRY MEASURES

metric	imperial
15g	½oz
30g	1oz
60g	2oz
90g	3oz
125g	4oz (¼lb)
155g	5oz
185g	6oz
220g	7oz
250g	8oz (½lb)
280g	9oz
315g	10oz
345g	11oz
375g	12oz (¾lb)
410g	13oz
440g	14oz
470g	15oz
500g	16oz (1lb)
750g	24oz (1½lb)
1kg	32oz (2lb)

LIQUID MEASURES

metric	imperial
30ml	1 fluid oz
60ml	2 fluid oz
100ml	3 fluid oz
125ml	4 fluid oz
150ml	5 fluid oz
190ml	6 fluid oz
250ml	8 fluid oz
300ml	10 fluid oz
500ml	16 fluid oz
600ml	20 fluid oz
1000ml (1 litre)	1¾ pints

LENGTH MEASURES

metric	imperial
3mm	⅛in
6mm	¼in
1cm	½in
2cm	¾in
2.5cm	1in
5cm	2in
6cm	2½in
8cm	3in
10cm	4in
13cm	5in
15cm	6in
18cm	7in
20cm	8in
22cm	9in
25cm	10in
28cm	11in
30cm	12in (1ft)

OVEN TEMPERATURES

The temperatures in this book and below are for fan-forced ovens; for conventional ovens, increase the temperature by 10-20 degrees.

	°C (Celsius)	°F (Fahrenheit)
Very slow	80	175
Slow	100	210
Moderately slow	130	260
Moderate	140	280
Moderately hot	160	325
Hot	180	350
Very hot	200	400

Measurements for cake pans are approximate only.
Using same-shaped cake pans of a similar size should not affect the outcome of your baking.
We measure the inside top of the cake pan to determine size.

Index

ARE MEDIA BOOKS

Chief executive officer Jane Huxley

General manager, homes & lifestyle Jocelin Abbey

Books director David Scotto

Creative director Hannah Blackmore

Project editor Stephanie Kistner

Food editor Bronwen Clark

Production controller Kara Stead

Author Kate Jenkinson

SHOOT TEAM

Photographer John Paul Urizar

Stylist Olivia Blackmore

Photochef Rebecca Lyall

Hair stylist & makeup artist Renee Sayed

Printed in China by
C&C Offset Printing Co. Ltd., China

A catalogue record for this book is available from the National Library of Australia.
ISBN 978-1-76122-221-4

Published by Are Media Books, a division of Are Media Pty Limited,54 Park St, Sydney; GPO Box 4088, Sydney, NSW 2001, Australia
Ph +61 2 9282 8000
www.aremediabooks.com.au

Published in 2026 by Are Media Books, Australia.
Are Media Books is a division of Are Media Pty Ltd.

ABOUT THE AUTHOR

Kate has been a popular face on film and television screens for over 20 years, starring in beloved shows like Offspring, Rush, NCIS, 5 Bedrooms, House Husbands and most recognisably as Allie Novak in the worldwide smash hit Wentworth.

Her popular online cooking series My Sh!t Kitchen has amassed over 400,000 followers across Instagram and TikTok and is the inspiration behind this cookbook.

Kate is a proud ambassador for imperfection. Her social media presence is a celebration of mediocrity and a rejection of the constant stream of impossibly perfect imagery we are fed daily through mainstream and social media.

Kate is raising her adorable sous chef Fletcher on the Gold Coast where she is patiently waiting for his fussy eating phase to pass. No luck as yet.

@KATEJENKO @KATEJENKO.TIKTOK

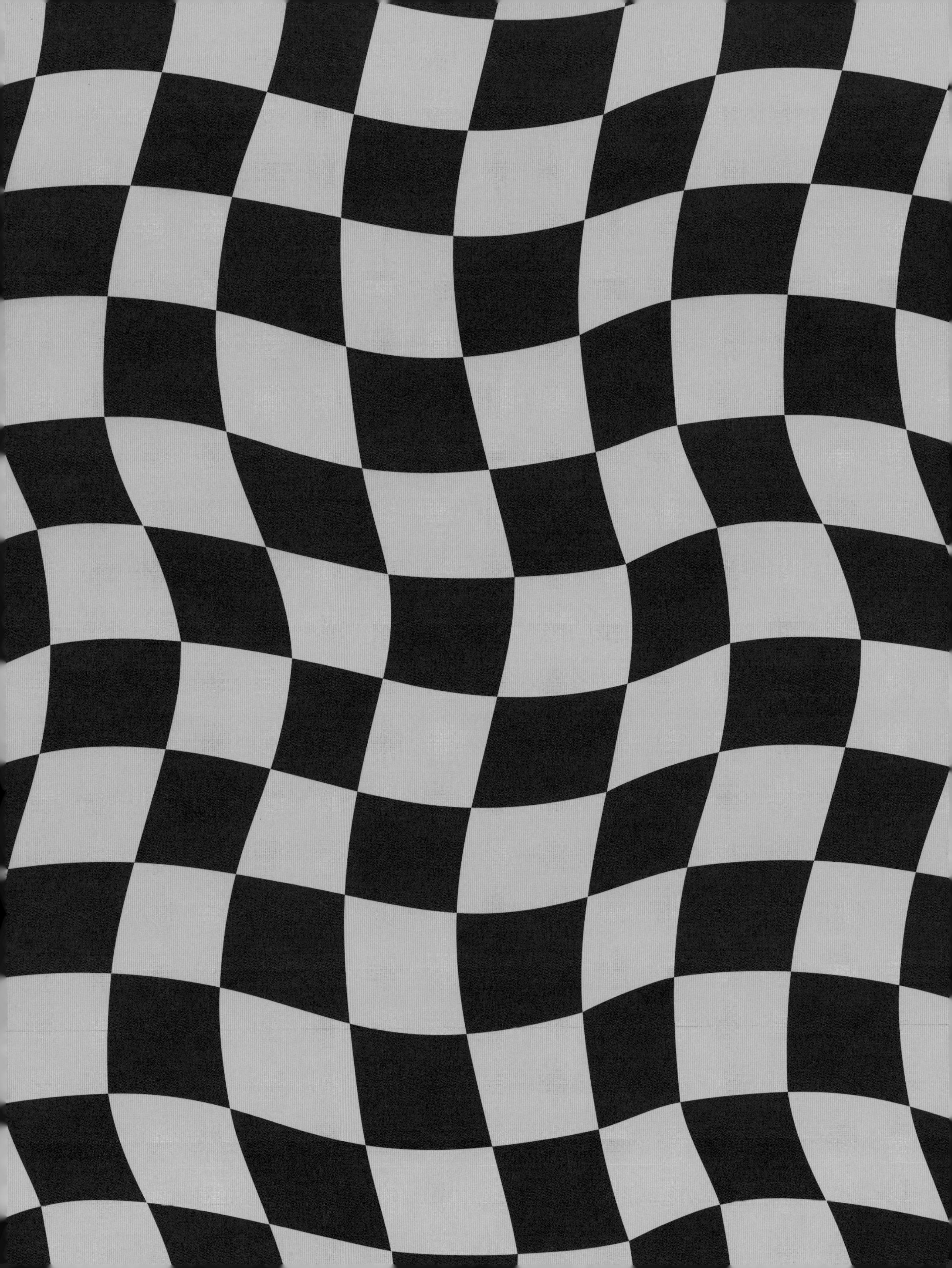